THE 30-DAY CHARACTER CHALLENGE

THE 30-DAY CHARACTER CHALLENGE

Robynn K. Coates

FireEscape Publishing ◆ Chanute, Kansas

Copyright © 2010 by Robynn K. Coates

The 30-Day Character Challenge

by Robynn K. Coates

Printed in the United States of America

ISBN 9780991164936

All rights reserved solely by the author. The author guarantees all contents are original and do not infringe upon the legal rights of any other person or work. No part of this book may be reproduced in any form without the permission of the author.

Unless otherwise indicated, Bible quotations are taken from the New International Version (NIV 2011). Copyright © 1978 by the Zondervan Corporation.

OTHER BIBLE TRANSLATIONS USED:

New International Version (NIV 1984) Copyright © 1984 by the Zondervan Corporation. New Living Translation (NLT) Copyright © 2005 by Tyndale House Publishers Inc. Amplified (AMP) Copyright © 2003 by the Zondervan Corporation and the Lockman Foundation. The Message (MSG) Copyright © 2002 by Eugene H. Peterson. King James Version (KJV). World English Bible (WEB) Public Domain, Translation, English Standard Version (ESV) Copyright © 2001 by the Wheaton: Good News Publishers.

FireEscape Publishing, LLC

Acknowledgements

To Michelle Johnson, for all your helpful comments and suggestions; and all those at First Baptist Church in Chanute, Kansas who gave input on this project.

Dedication

*Dedicated to Scott, Sophia, and Isabella.
You inspire me to live with character.*

CONTENTS

Introduction
Day 1:	Purpose of This Challenge	1
Day 2:	Truth about Self	7
Day 3:	Commitment to Change	11
Day 4:	Adopt a N.O.W. Philosophy (No Opportunity Wasted)	15
Day 5:	Motive	17
Day 6:	Admit You Are Helpless on Your Own	19
Day 7:	Personal Integrity Audit	23
Day 8:	Do Not Despise the Day of Small Beginnings	27
Day 9:	Resolve	31
Day 10:	Stewardship Fitness Test	33
Day 11:	Walking in Truth	45
Day 12:	Is Your Word Your Bond?	49
Day 13:	Self-Control	53
Day 14:	Self-Control: Thoughts	59
Day 15:	Self-Control: Words	65
Day 16:	Self-Control: Actions	77
Day 17:	Obedience Out of a Pure Heart	87
Day 18:	Appropriate Boundary Lines	91
Day 19:	Guard Your Heart	95
Day 20:	No Compromise: Living by Your Conscience	99
Day 21:	Patience	103
Day 22:	Perseverance	105
Day 23:	Faithfulness	107
Day 24:	Love	111
Day 25:	Companions	113
Day 26:	Pride	115
Day 27:	Greed	119
Day 28:	Are You Committed to Being a Lifelong Learner?	121
Day 29:	What Kind of Person Will You Be in Five Years?	123
Day 30:	Baseline Data	125

INTRODUCTION

* * *

Are you a man or woman of character? Think about that for a moment. If you had to judge yourself in this category on a scale of one to ten, what number would you assign yourself? What number would others assign to you? What number would God give you?

As believers, we are given the mandate to develop our character. I like to call 2 Peter the "Character Chapter of the Bible." Take a look at what the Message Bible says regarding character in chapter 1, verses 5-9:

> ***So don't lose a minute in building on what you've been given, complementing your basic faith with good character, spiritual understanding, alert discipline, passionate patience, reverent wonder, warm friendliness, and generous love, each dimension fitting into and developing the others. With these qualities active and growing in your lives, no grass will grow under your feet, no day will pass without its reward as you mature in your experience of our Master Jesus. Without these qualities you can't see what's right before you, oblivious that your old sinful life has been wiped off the books.***

What does your character, your inner life, look like? Are you "oblivious that your old sinful life has been wiped off the books" and therefore live in defeat, discouragement, and disappointment? If you desire to live a victorious Christian life, you must be a man or woman of character. This is by no means an all-inclusive study on character, but it is definitely a start. At times, the process may seem overwhelming, but keep in mind the promise we have in Philippians 1:6:

Being confident of this, that he who began a good work in you will carry it on to completion until the day of Christ Jesus.

Tired of the status quo? Want to live with purpose? Accept the challenge and change your course starting today!

DAY 1
PURPOSE OF THIS CHALLENGE

My dear children, for whom I am again in the pains of childbirth until Christ is formed in you.
Galatians 4:19

* * *

What is the "Content" of Your Character?

Are you ready for the greatest challenge of your life? Its implications will literally change the footprints you leave on history. As I was writing this book, I read in my local paper about a professional baseball player who admitted to steroid use. The article quoted that he "sobbed and sniffled, giving the missing answer to the steroids question." His following statement dittos what is true in the lives of many people, "The toughest thing is my wife, my parents, close friends have had no idea that I hid it from them all this time."[1]

The sad reality is that this kind of story has become the norm. We have become accustomed to them, so our children live in a society in which character is a bygone commodity. In our culture, what you have on the outside is more important than what you have on the inside. Unfortunately, the younger generations of our country have never witnessed a time when we placed more stock in character than in outward appearances.

How about you? What is the content of your character? Do you fall into the same category as the baseball player, masquerading like an actor, presenting a life very different from what is really going on?

We desperately need men and women who will stand up and be people of character. Fortunately, if you are willing to take on this challenge, you have the perfect role model: Jesus

Christ. It is His character that we will examine and try to emulate. The standard is high, but its rewards are great. Seem impossible? It is, in your own strength. But don't worry, because you have a helper, the Holy Spirit, who will supply the strength you need. He will take you where you need to go, if you'll cooperate with him.

> **For it is God which worketh in you both to will and to do of his good pleasure.**
> Philippians 2:13 (KJV)

What exactly is character, anyway? The Merriam-Webster dictionary defines character as "the complex of mental and ethical traits marking a person or group."[2] My favorite definition of character is that of Russell W. Gough in his book, *Character Is Destiny*. He defines character as "the sum total of your habits, your personal assortment of virtues and vices."[3]

Your character is defined by (but is not limited to) your choices:
- Truthful OR dishonest
- Loving OR unloving
- Kind OR unkind
- Respectful OR disrespectful
- A person of your word OR someone whose talk is cheap
- Self-controlled in all areas OR impulsive, with desires you can't control
- Patient OR impatient
- Faithful in fulfilling commitments OR unfaithful in fulfilling commitments
- Humble OR proud
- A good steward with money OR a poor money manager
- A good steward with time OR someone who wastes and misuses time

- Kind and appropriate with words OR rude in speech, a gossiper, and unkind with words
- One whose thoughts are controlled and pure OR one with an uncontrolled thought life, including impure thoughts and lack of self-control
- A doer OR a big talker, never following through on plans
- One who thinks the little things are important OR one who dismisses the little things (Despising the day of small things—Zechariah 4:10, KJV)
- Unselfish OR selfish, thinking about only yourself

This list describes who you are—your character. How does yours stack up? Let me issue a warning at this point: This challenge will mess with your life. Nothing is off limits and nothing will go untouched because that is, after all, your character—the deepest part of you. No doubt, you have good qualities. That's great. But the truth is that maybe you're more defined by those qualities that aren't so great—those characteristics that you would like to sweep under the rug and forget about. Those qualities that gnaw on you and keep you imprisoned. Maybe the people around you are quite aware of them. Maybe they're your deepest secrets. Regardless, they are the true picture of "you."

Now, if you're like most people, that may be a depressing and discouraging thought. Taking an honest look at oneself can be disheartening and downright scary. I think that might be one reason character is glossed over and ignored. Bottom line: it's hard work and it takes time. It requires you to roll up your sleeves and deal with issues that aren't comfortable and certainly aren't convenient. And because of this, it's not popular.

Take a look at the industries that promote image and that influence us regarding what's "in" and what's "out". Hollywood and the media place little, if any, emphasis on character. We continually hear stories of fame, fortune, and "success," but when you take a deeper look at these individuals' private lives, you often find them plagued by infidelity, drug abuse, or other destructive behaviors.

Sadly, what these people and the majority of the people watching them don't understand is that you will go only as far as your greatest weakness. It's as if your weaknesses are a restraining leash attached to a collar around your neck. For each person, that leash is a different length. For some it's short, for others it's longer, but regardless, eventually that leash will jerk you back when you've reached its limit.

You can live within the confines of this leash. The comfort factor may be higher for you than for another, but bottom line: you are on a leash. How sad to be on your deathbed, thinking about your many accomplishments, only to realize that the one thing you failed to master was yourself. As a result, you've left a string of broken relationships and missed opportunities in the wake.

At this point you may be tempted to close the book and ask, "Why bother?" Maybe you see mastering yourself as impossible. Maybe you've tried to overcome an addiction, character flaw, or behavior for the "nth" time, and you're realistic enough to know you can't do it on your own.

Here's the good news: you have a helper. Jesus Christ came to set the captive free (Isaiah 61:1). That was His purpose. This freedom is available to you right now. Which one describes you?

1. A non-believer who has not been set free from sin
2. A believer who has been set free from sin, but is struggling with walking out the freedom Christ died to give you
3. A believer of Jesus Christ who is walking in freedom

When we surrender our lives to Christ, we are set free from sin. However, learning how to walk out that freedom takes time. Freedom comes in stages and in degrees. The more you learn about God, his Word, and how to apply it, the more you will walk in freedom.

If you have not yet taken the first step to freedom, receiving Jesus Christ as your Lord and Savior, today is your day. It's simple. Romans 10:9-10 says, "If you declare with your mouth, 'Jesus is Lord,' and believe in your heart that God raised him from the dead, you will be saved. For it is with your heart that you believe and are justified, and it is with your mouth that you profess your faith and are saved."

Once you take this step, you receive the awesome benefits that God has promised to those who believe. Let this scripture encourage you as you embark on the most important endeavor you can pursue: developing your character.

His divine power has given us everything we need for a godly life through our knowledge of him who called us by his own glory and goodness.
2 Peter 1:3

In starting *The 30-Day Character Challenge*, I originally wanted to say that the only requirement is a willingness to change. But then I began to think I'm not sure that's even a requirement. I know some of us are harder nuts to crack than others and we are all at different places in life. My prayer is that God will use this study, regardless of where you are on the Ready-To-Change-and-Master-Myself pendulum. Maybe you are desperate for a change and ripe for the pickin'. Great. Maybe you're on the outside looking in, testing the water to see if this "character thing" is for you. That's great as well. I pray God meets you in an incredible way, right where you are.

If you want to get the most out of this challenge, participation is necessary. This simply means asking yourself the tough questions and being willing to face up to the truth.

I also highly recommend having an accountability partner you can go through this challenge with. Choose someone you can be 100 percent honest with and whom you can trust.

    I also encourage you to keep a journal. This would be a great place to write down the assignments and your thoughts about them as well as the changes you see in your life. You will also be asked to grade yourself on different aspects of your character. When doing so, take a look at the last six months of your life, and rate yourself accordingly. This will be your baseline and give you a starting point.

    Finally, resolve to see this study through to its completion. You will be challenged, disappointed, and deflated at times. Remember, God is working everything for your good and will strengthen you in this journey. Be strong and courageous! Pursue character with reckless abandon.

Challenge #1

Take time to note one person you can rely on to hold you accountable.

My accountability partner:
_____

Let's get started!

SOUL SEARCH AND RATE YOURSELF OVER THE PAST SIX MONTHS
DAY 1: Are you a person of character?

Go to the Baseline Data Table on DAY 30 and rate yourself.

DAY 2
TRUTH ABOUT SELF

Behold, You desire truth in the inner being; make me therefore to know wisdom in my inmost heart.
Psalm 51:6 (AMP)

* * *

The first step we must take in *The 30-Day Character Challenge* is to embrace truth, specifically truth about ourselves. Sure, we enjoy hearing how great we are in certain areas or how talented, selfless, good-looking, smart, or loving we are, but how about those areas we are ashamed of or aren't all that concerned with? Maybe the problem is that we don't want to deal with certain issues in our lives. Maybe we have deep hurts, secret sins, or character inconveniences we don't want to face up to. It's easier to blame and make excuses: "I can't help it I'm so blatantly honest." "My father was like that, and so was his father." And the list goes on.

Let's be real. The truth hurts, especially when that truth is about us. But the truth also liberates us when we acknowledge what's true about us and then align ourselves with God's truth through obedience. I'll give a personal example.

After teaching high school for six years, I needed a change. Still wanting to work with kids, but not necessarily in the classroom setting, I choose to get my masters in school counseling. Since I live in rural Kansas, my options were limited. The best choice at that time was Liberty University in Virginia. The program was online with the exception of four classes I would need to take on campus. Each of these on-campus classes was an intensive class crammed into one week.

Being on campus and around other students and professors was exciting for me. I always came to class prepared and ready to discuss the material of the day. The problem was that I was over-excited to share the information I had learned. I also had teaching experience from which to draw. As a result of my over-exuberance, I talked too much, often monopolizing the class discussion.

No one ever called me on it. However, God wasn't willing to overlook my selfishness and pride. And trust me, He got His point across to me. Correction is never fun. It's embarrassing, humbling, and uncomfortable. But the Bible says it brings righteousness and peace if we allow ourselves to be trained by it (Hebrews 12:11).

I also remember a vocal class I took in my senior year of high school. I was a popular student who was influential and, for the most part, a good example to other students. However, for some reason, this particular day I was being very non-cooperative with the teacher. In front of the entire class, I challenged my teacher in a way that undermined his authority. Another teacher, whom the rest of the students and I admired and respected greatly, was sitting in the back of the class. After hearing my lack of respect and cooperation, she came to my music teacher's defense and rebuked me in front of the entire class. I felt about an inch tall, but I deserved what I got.

What qualities about yourself do you need to be man or woman enough to face up to, own up to, and take responsibility for? (Isn't that really what we mean when we talk about being a person of character?) If you need help identifying areas, refer to the descriptive list of what our character consists of on DAY 1.

Can you be honest enough to take the first step to change? If your answer to that question is "Yes," then you have an awesome promise:

For we do not have a High Priest Who is unable to understand and sympathize and have a shared feeling with our weaknesses and infirmities and liability to the assaults of temptation, but One who

> *has been tempted in every respect as we are, yet without sinning. Let us then fearlessly and confidently and boldly draw near to the throne of grace (the throne of God's unmerited favor to us sinners), that we may receive mercy [for our failures] and find grace to help in good time for every need [appropriate help and well-timed help, coming just when we need it].*
> Hebrews 4:15-16 (AMP)

Will you fearlessly, confidently, and boldly draw near to God and receive His mercy and His help? He's waiting.

Challenge #2

Be completely honest with yourself. Ask God to show you where your character comes up short. Allow Him to strip you down to your core. No defenses, no charades, no pretenses, no masks—just you and God. This is true self-examination. There's no longer any reason to hide, justify, or make excuses. He loves you unconditionally, just as you are, but as the saying goes, "loves you too much to let you stay there." You may have a long way to go, but He'll walk beside you every step of the way. Write a prayer to God, telling Him the truth about your struggles and weaknesses. Or, if you're like me and love to use textual bullets, make a list of them.

Ask God for His help and for courage as He shines His light, revealing changes you need to make. Dave Ramsey, financial guru, often talks about changing your family tree. When you make the commitment to being a person of character, that's exactly what you are doing—changing your family tree. Your choice will have a lasting effect on you and those around you, as well.

The righteous man walks in his integrity; blessed (happy, fortunate, enviable) are his children after him.
Proverbs 20:7 (AMP)

_____
_____
_____
_____
_____
_____
_____
_____
_____
_____

Are you willing to let God reveal your shortcomings, flaws, and failures? Are you willing to allow Him to expose the deepest parts of your heart? Will you then be willing to face them and deal with them?

Search me, O God, and know my heart; test me and know my anxious thoughts.
Psalm 139:23 (NIV 1984)

SOUL SEARCH AND RATE YOURSELF THE PAST SIX MONTHS
DAY 2: Are you willing to face the truth about yourself?

Go to the Baseline Data Table on DAY 30 and rate yourself

DAY 3
COMMITMENT TO CHANGE
(And Sticking to It until the Mission is Complete)

No discipline seems pleasant at the time, but painful. Later on, however, it produces a harvest of righteousness and peace for those who have been trained by it.
Hebrews 12:11

* * *

There is nothing easy, convenient, or instant about character development. It is painstaking and requires delayed gratification, which is why so few enlist. But the rewards are incredible.

Hebrews 12:11 tells us that discipline produces righteousness and peace. What's so great about righteousness and peace? For starters, who doesn't want to be right? I know people don't always define it that way, but think about it for a moment. There is a desire in all of us to measure up, to be "okay." We may not translate it as a desire for righteousness, but it exists in all of us and is expressed in many different ways.

Most people live with a nagging sense that something isn't right with them. As a result, they try their best to make themselves right. Some try to measure up through performance on the job or in other areas, such as sports, music—you name it. Accomplishment gives others a sense of affirmation. This could be on the job or in their personal life. Maybe they run marathons, climb mountains, try to be the first person to ... (You fill in the blank). Still others think being in the right social circle or having lots of friends is the ticket to being "right" and validated.

None of these things are bad, per se. In fact, many of them can be advantageous, helping us grow and develop as people. The question is, why are you doing what you're doing? Is it for personal growth or is it because you think that once you accomplish your goal, you will finally be okay, acceptable, or worthy of love and respect?

Being right with God is all those things. It's total acceptance and unconditional love. It's receiving the stamp of approval and, best of all, getting it from God. When you truly understand what being righteous (right with God) means, you no longer have to try to prove yourself. The pressure is taken off. Instead of always trying to "do" you can finally just "be."

Being right with God leads to peace. Peace with God, peace with others, and peace with yourself. I believe peace is one of the most sought-after commodities of mankind. You may be shaking your head, saying, "No, it's success, money, fame, recognition, power." But consider this: why do people go after all those things? Isn't it ultimately because they think those things will make them feel better? That they will bring contentment, happiness, acceptance—in a nutshell, peace?

Unfortunately, many people reach their pinnacle to find that the thing they were really seeking—peace—has eluded them. We see it all too often in the world of sports, politics, and stardom. These individuals reach the top and then almost predictably, many of them self-destruct in front of the entire world. They are no different than most; they just live their life in the public's eye, so their fall seems much more devastating.

When righteousness and peace become your objective, your priorities change and your life is dramatically affected. Are you ready to make the commitment to be transformed, along with the commitment to see it through?

If so, sign and date the following contract. From this point on, commit to being a person of character. The past is behind. No matter what you have done up to this point, you have the power of choice. You can be a person of character. It's up to you.

Challenge #3

Sign the following contract with yourself. It may help to photocopy your signed contract and display it in a conspicuous place.

I, _____,
on _____ of 20_____, commit to being a person of character and will endeavor always to that end.
Signed
_____

SOUL SEARCH AND RATE YOURSELF THE PAST SIX MONTHS
DAY 3: Are you committed to becoming a person of character?

Go to the Baseline Data Table on DAY 30 and rate yourself.

Day 4
ADOPT A N.O.W. PHILOSOPHY
(No Opportunity Wasted)

Look carefully then how you walk! Live purposefully and worthily and accurately, not as the unwise and witless, but as wise (sensible, intelligent people), making the very most of the time [buying up each opportunity], because the days are evil.
Ephesians 5:15-16 (AMP)

* * *

People of character are in the habit of living in the moment. They place importance on every opportunity, whether these opportunities seem significant or insignificant.

If you tend to be more of a dreamer than a doer, have problems with procrastination, or struggle with laziness and/or lack of self-control, you may find this challenge difficult. Your thought process might go something like this: "I may as well blow it since I made a mistake. I'll start over tomorrow," or "I'll start focusing on my goals on January 1." You have big plans and goals, but you put them off until tomorrow or a more convenient time. This mindset will steal your life from you as you obliviously sit back and let your life slip by.

It's easy to rationalize passing up less-than-ideal opportunities in hopes that conditions will be more conducive in the near future. The problem is that these ideal conditions never transpire. Maybe the opportunity you're passing up is quality time with your spouse, children, or other family members. Maybe today you can't invest a good hour, but invest what time you do have whether that's five minutes or thirty. Maybe your opportunity is giving your time or money to a good cause, speaking a kind word, using a talent to help others, starting a business, fulfilling your commitment to yourself regarding eating right and exercising, or choosing to walk in self-control instead of giving in to your weakness or addiction.

In Deuteronomy, God exhorted the Israelites with a "NOW" command:

> ***Hear, O Israel. You are to cross the Jordan today to go in to dispossess nations greater and mightier than you are, cities great and fortified up to the heavens.***
> Deuteronomy 9:1 (AMP)

Challenge #4

Grade yourself on how you use your time and the opportunities presented to you. Do you look at every day as an opportunity to grow and learn, or do you simply exist and blow the opportunities given to you?

What grade did you receive? _____

SOUL SEARCH AND RATE YOURSELF THE PAST SIX MONTHS
DAY 4: Do you take advantage of every moment?

Go to the Baseline Data Table on DAY 30 and rate yourself.

DAY 5
MOTIVE

__Flee the evil desires of youth and pursue righteousness, faith, love and peace, along with those who call on the Lord out of a pure heart.__
2 Timothy 2:22

* * *

As you take *The 30-Day Character Challenge*, ask yourself, "What is my motive?" You can do all the right things, but if you don't have the right motive, your efforts are in vain. Are you endeavoring to be a person of character out of a pure heart? Having the right motives is important to God. In 1 Samuel, God rejects King Saul, even though it appears he has it all on the outside. God's response was:

__… Do not consider his appearance or his height, for I have rejected him. The Lord does not look at the things people look at. People look at the outward appearance, but the Lord looks at the heart.__
1 Samuel 16:7

Examine your heart. What are your motives? Circle the ones that apply:

PURE	IMPURE
Unselfish	Selfishness
Humility	Pride
Focused on Others	"It's All About Me!"

If you've taken a good look at your motives and don't like what you see, take heart. God offered us His help in the book of Ezekiel:

I will sprinkle clean water on you, and you will be clean; I will cleanse you from all your impurities and from all your idols. I will give you a new heart and put a new spirit in you; I will remove from you your heart of stone and give you a heart of flesh. And I will put my Spirit in you and move you to follow my decrees and be careful to keep my laws.
Ezekiel 36:25-27

Challenge #5

Answer this simple question: Are your motives right?

                YES   NO

If your answer is no, are you willing to change?

SOUL SEARCH AND RATE YOURSELF THE PAST SIX MONTHS
DAY 5: When God looks at your heart, what does He see?

Go to the Baseline Data Table on DAY 30 and rate yourself.

DAY 6
ADMIT YOU ARE HELPLESS ON YOUR OWN

[Not in your own strength] for it is God Who is all the while effectually at work in you [energizing and creating in you the power and desire], both to will and to work for His good pleasure and satisfaction and delight.
Philippians 2:13 (AMP)

* * *

This challenge is specifically for the "stud." (Pardon the expression, especially if it's not one you would use. I was a teenager in the 80s, and that was the terminology we used then. Please feel free to submit your own descriptive adjective.)

If you're a stud, you know it and so does everyone else. If you just think you're a stud, this applies to you as well. (It applies to everyone to some degree or another.) From my experience, people are coined "stud" (or whatever the "in" word is at the time) due to athletic ability, good looks, and possibly a good personality and intelligence. Let me challenge that definition with this one: A stud/studess is someone who has mastered his thoughts, words, and actions. In other words, he has mastered himself.

I'm not talking about putting a lid on one's impulses and desires, hoping the pressurized tank doesn't blow any time soon. I'm talking about self-control. Do you have it? Self-control is not denying that you have these impulses and desires. Instead, it's understanding that left unchecked, those impulses will wreak havoc in your life. And then you deal with them appropriately. Maybe at this point, you are thinking, "Yes, I agree, but how do I deal with them?"

If you enjoy futile activities (which I'm certain you don't), continue trying to master them on your own, white-knuckling your way through life. If you choose this route, it will be as effective as banging your head against the wall.

I should know because I've spent years taking that approach. I know all about beating my head against the wall. I've done it many times—trying to master myself on my own. It never worked. Then came the guilt and self-condemnation that said, "How could I be so stupid? Why didn't I learn the first time around? When will I ever learn?"

If this describes you, use it to your advantage. The learning curve can be accelerated for you when you realize your way doesn't work, so you're ready to move on to a method that does work.

Now, if you are one who thinks you're "all that," this may be hard to hear. The truth hurts, after all, but it will set you free. And here's the truth: You can't do it on your own. Maybe you're thinking, "Yes, I know," or maybe you're in denial. Either way, it's true, and no amount of rationalizing, dismissing, or disagreeing will change that fact. So, what are you going to do about it? The teacher in me will list your options in a multiple-choice format:

A. Keep banging your head against the wall through denial.
B. Keep banging your head against the wall by ignoring the problem.
C. Keep banging your head against the wall, thinking you just need to try harder.
D. Enough of beating your head against the wall. Realize you can't do this on your own. You need help!

If you chose D, you are ready to move on and embark on the noblest aspiration one could undertake—becoming a person of character. Fasten your seatbelt; you are about to take the ride of your life.

Challenge # 6

This challenge involves admitting your helplessness and your need for God's intervention. He has promised He would send the Holy Spirit to be our Helper.

Let us then approach God's throne of grace with confidence, so that we may receive mercy and find grace to help us in our time of need.
Hebrews 4:16

How do you receive help from God? The following will get you started:

- Acknowledge your dependency on Him.
- Ask for help frequently; spend time talking to God in prayer.
- Spend time daily reading the Bible.
- Attend and get involved in a Bible-believing church.
- Find someone you can be accountable to and can share your struggles and victories with.

This challenge puts you face-to-face with God, admitting your inability to master yourself on your own and asking for His help. Don't know how to begin? "Help, God!" is a great place to start. If you want to, write out your prayer in the following space:

_____
_____
_____
_____
_____

SOUL SEARCH AND RATE YOURSELF THE PAST SIX MONTHS
DAY 6: Are you willing to admit your helplessness and receive help from God?

Go to the Baseline Data Table on DAY 30 and rate yourself.

DAY 7
PERSONAL INTEGRITY AUDIT

I know, my God, that you test the heart and are pleased with integrity.
1 Chronicles 29:17a

* * *

A key quality in a person of character is integrity. And a key quality of integrity is doing what you say you're going to do. Are you a person of your word? Are you willing to fulfill your commitment regardless of the cost? Hold up the mirror and take a look at how you fare. Sobering? Probably. No one said this would be easy. But it will be worth it. And you will absolutely, positively not regret the sacrifice when your payday comes.

You're the one who has to live with yourself. Being able to look in the mirror and see a person of integrity and honor looking back at you is priceless.

Are you willing to be that person?

Challenge #7

Rate your integrity from 1-10 (1 being low, 10 being high) in keeping your promises to yourself and others.

Keeping promises to yourself (Doing what you say you will do)

1   2   3   4   5   6   7   8   9   10

Keeping promises to others (fulfilling your commitments and following through on what you say you will do; i.e., promises to kids, spouse, family, church or volunteer organizations, meeting your financial obligations on time. Saying "Let's get together," and following through)

    1   2   3   4   5   6   7   8   9   10

Once you have determined your level of integrity, specify those areas that lack integrity:

1. _____
2. _____
3. _____
4. _____
5. _____
6. _____
7. _____
8. _____
9. _____

Now for each area, list the first step you are going to take to begin walking in integrity:

1. _____
2. _____
3. _____
4. _____
5. _____
6. _____
7. _____
8. _____
9. _____

SOUL SEARCH AND RATE YOURSELF THE PAST SIX MONTHS
DAY 7: How do you score on a personal-integrity audit?

Go to the Baseline Data Table on DAY 30 and rate yourself.

DAY 8
DO NOT DESPISE THE DAY OF SMALL BEGINNINGS

... Does anyone dare despise this day of small beginnings ...?
Zechariah 4:10 (The Message)

Do not despise these small beginnings....
Zechariah 4:10 (NLT)

* * *

Sometimes I just don't get it. Yes, I admit I can be clueless at times. I have been around sports and music enough to know that to master a skill, you must break it down into small, incremental steps that build upon each other. But when it comes to my personal life, such as forming a new habit, I have the all-or-nothing mindset. I expect perfection immediately. And when I don't succeed at the goal I set out to achieve, I beat myself up over not being able to keep my word to myself.

The problem is that I wasn't willing to take small steps. Instead, I wanted immediate success. It's like going to the first day of basketball practice and expecting to make ten lay-ups in a row. Now, if you play in the NBA, college, or maybe even high school, that may not be too difficult, but if you're a beginner and have that goal, you're setting yourself up for failure. To succeed, you must break it down.

Where have you had difficulty keeping your word to yourself and others? Relationships? Work/family balance? Exercise and eating right? Financial accountability? Overcoming a bad habit or addiction? Implementing a new habit? Ask yourself why you haven't fulfilled your commitment. Maybe it's because you refuse to take small steps. If you need the motivation of having a big goal with big expectations, by all means, give it a try. Sometimes that approach works because it overcomes inertia and gives immediate momentum and results. But if you are hacking away at the same old goal, maybe breaking it down is your key to success. Imagine how much you could change in just one year if you are willing to take one small step after another.

Challenge #8

In the two tables that follow, choose the goal directly in front of you, preferably the one that is most important to you. Then list the small steps you can begin to take immediately. Include a completion date for all your steps and a list of the character traits necessary to fulfill your goal. Finally, include steps you will need to take to acquire these traits.

GOAL	
STEPS	DATE
1	
2	
3	
4	
5	
6	
7	
8	
9	
10	
11	

Character Traits Necessary to Achieve Goals and Steps to Acquire These Traits		
1.)		
STEPS	A.	
	B.	
	C.	
	D.	
2.)		
STEPS	A.	
	B.	
	C.	
	D.	
3.)		
STEPS	A.	
	B.	
	C.	
	D.	

SOUL SEARCH AND RATE YOURSELF THE PAST SIX MONTHS
DAY 8: Are you willing to take small steps?

Go to the Baseline Data Table on DAY 30 and rate yourself.

DAY 9
RESOLVE

You have proved my heart.
You have visited me in the night.
You have tried me, and found nothing.
I have resolved that my mouth shall not disobey.
Psalm 17:3 (WEB)

* * *

How would you like to be known as a man/woman after God's heart? Although King David is known for some enormous failures (adultery and then murder), he is referred to in the Bible as a man after God's heart. Yes, he had a major lapse in judgment, which cost him dearly, but that wasn't David's defining moment. Rather, he goes down in history as a man who pursued the heartbeat of God. The following prayer of David's, found in Psalm 101, is just another example of his commitment and resolve to live a blameless life:

I will be careful to lead a blameless life— when will you come to me? I will conduct the affairs of my house with a blameless heart. I will not look with approval on anything that is vile. I hate what faithless people do; I will have no part in it.
Psalm 101:2-3

Challenge #9

Becoming a person of character won't happen automatically. You will need resolve, a digging in of the heels that says, "I'm determined to lead a blameless life." Have you made that resolve? If not, are you ready to do so?

Yes, I'm Ready ____   No, I'm Not Ready ____

SOUL SEARCH AND RATE YOURSELF THE PAST SIX MONTHS
DAY 9: Are you determined to lead a righteous life, regardless of the cost?

Go to the Baseline Data Table on DAY 30 and rate yourself.

DAY 10
STEWARDSHIP FITNESS TEST

Do you not know that your bodies are temples of the Holy Spirit, who is in you, whom you have received from God? You are not your own; you were bought at a price. Therefore honor God with your bodies.
1 Corinthians 6:19-20

* * *

Being a person of character is about stewardship. We don't hear much of stewardship these days, at least not in our culture. In fact, many people may not even know what stewardship means, which is unfortunate because stewardship will define you as a person and chart your course. Contrary to what many believe, we do not live and die unto ourselves. The Bible says in Romans 14:12 that we all will have to give an account for the way we lived our lives. You may never have heard this before, but you are not your own.

You are a steward. A steward is not the boss. A steward is a manager and is given the responsibility to do just that—manage. How are you doing in that regard? If you sit back and evaluate the way you manage the different aspects of your life, what grade do you get? Would you hire someone like yourself to manage your affairs, or would you hand out a pink slip? Many people are baffled as to why they aren't progressing and being promoted. They think they deserve better, but when the truth is told, they are not being faithful with what's been entrusted to them. Luke 16:10-12 tells us,

Whoever can be trusted with very little can also be trusted with much, and whoever is dishonest with very little will also be dishonest with much. So if you have not been trustworthy in handling worldly

wealth, who will trust you with true riches? And if you have not been trustworthy with someone else's property, who will give you property of your own?

If you have ever played sports or started a fitness program, your coach probably gave you a fitness test on day one. It wasn't meant to discourage you into quitting, but rather it gave you a baseline of your fitness level. Later, as your season or program progressed, you likely took that same test again to show your improvement. The harder you worked, the greater the results.

Challenge #10

The following activity is a "fitness test" for your stewardship. You will rate the following areas that you are responsible for. Rate yourself from 1-10 (10 being high). As you work on character development, re-rate yourself from time to time. It will be a good indicator of where you are and where you need to go.

SPIRITUAL: How are you doing in those areas that affect your spiritual wellbeing?

Prayer:

1   2   3   4   5   6   7   8   9   10

Devote yourselves to prayer, being watchful and thankful.
Colossians 4:2

Bible Study:

1   2   3   4   5   6   7   8   9   10

This Book of the Law shall not depart out of your mouth, but you shall meditate on it day and night, that you may observe and do according to all that is written in it. For then you shall make your way prosperous, and then you shall deal wisely and have good success.
Joshua 1:8 (AMP)

Church Attendance:

1   2   3   4   5   6   7   8   9   10

Let us not give up meeting together, as some are in the habit of doing, but let us encourage one another—and all the more as you see the Day approaching.
Hebrews 10:25 (NIV 1984)

Service: Are you planted and plugged in? If you serve in more than one area, please rate each area.

_____

1   2   3   4   5   6   7   8   9   10

_____

1   2   3   4   5   6   7   8   9   10

_____

   1   2   3   4   5   6   7   8   9   10

The righteous will flourish like a palm tree, they will grow like a cedar of Lebanon; planted in the house of the Lord, they will flourish in the courts of our God.
Psalm 92:12-13

PERSONAL:

Time:

   1   2   3   4   5   6   7   8   9   10

Look carefully then how you walk! Live purposefully and worthily and accurately, not as the unwise and witless, but as wise (sensible, intelligent people), making the very most of the time [buying up each opportunity], because the days are evil.
Ephesians 5:15-16 (AMP)

Recreation, Hobbies and Free time:

Not only is recreation good; it is necessary. However, are your choices contributing to your personal growth and character, or are they time-wasters that cause you to compromise your convictions and principles?

     List the hobbies and activities you participate in when you have down time. You may be surprised to see that you are spending your time on meaningless and unfruitful activities such as gossiping with your girlfriends, watching hours of questionable television, eating because you're bored, etc.

_____
_____
_____
_____
_____
_____
_____
_____

1   2   3   4   5   6   7   8   9   10

And whatever you do, whether in word or deed, do it all in the name of the Lord Jesus, giving thanks to God the Father through him.
Colossians 3:17

Words:

1   2   3   4   5   6   7   8   9   10

… Whoever would love life and see good days must keep their tongue from evil and their lips from deceitful speech.
1 Peter 3:10

Home, Cars, and Possessions:

1   2   3   4   5   6   7   8   9   10

So if you have not been trustworthy in handling worldly wealth, who will trust you with true riches?
Luke 16:11

FINANCIAL:

Personal Finances:

    1   2   3   4   5   6   7   8   9   10

Tithing and Giving:

    1   2   3   4   5   6   7   8   9   10

"'Will a man rob God? Yet you rob me. But you ask, "How do we rob you?" In tithes and offerings. You are under a curse—the whole nation of you—because you are robbing me. Bring the whole tithe into the storehouse, that there may be food in my house. Test me in this,' says the Lord Almighty, 'and see if I will not throw open the floodgates of heaven and pour out so much blessing that you will not have room enough for it.'"
Malachi 3:8-10 (NIV 1984)

Planning For the Future:

    1   2   3   4   5   6   7   8   9   10

You still the hunger of those you cherish; their sons have plenty, and they store up wealth for their children.
Psalm 17:14b, (NIV 1984)

A good person leaves an inheritance for their children's children, but a sinner's wealth is stored up for the righteous.
Proverbs 13:22

Dishonest money dwindles away, but whoever gathers money little by little makes it grow.
Proverbs 13:11

SOCIAL/EMOTIONAL:

<u>Your role as a:</u>
<u>Spouse</u>

1   2   3   4   5   6   7   8   9   10

<u>Parent</u>

1   2   3   4   5   6   7   8   9   10

<u>Family Member</u>

1   2   3   4   5   6   7   8   9   10

<u>Friend</u>

1   2   3   4   5   6   7   8   9   10

PROFESSIONAL:

<u>On-the-Job Ethics:</u> Do you misrepresent yourself in business transactions, hours put in, etc.?

    1   2   3   4   5   6   7   8   9   10

<u>Work Ethic:</u>

    1   2   3   4   5   6   7   8   9   10

<u>Trustworthiness:</u>

    1   2   3   4   5   6   7   8   9   10

<u>Loyalty to the Company You Have Chosen to Work For:</u>

    1   2   3   4   5   6   7   8   9   10

PHYSICAL:

<u>Healthy Lifestyle:</u> Do you treat your body as a temple of the Holy Spirit and protect it from dangerous and hurtful chemicals, substances, and activities?

    1   2   3   4   5   6   7   8   9   10

> ***Do you not know that your body is a temple of the Holy Spirit, who is in you, whom you have received from God? You are not your own.***
> 1 Corinthians 6:19 (NIV 1984)

Exercise:

1   2   3   4   5   6   7   8   9   10

Eating Right:

1   2   3   4   5   6   7   8   9   10

SEXUAL:

Purity: Faithfulness to spouse in thoughts, words, and actions. If single, abstinence from sexual immorality.

1   2   3   4   5   6   7   8   9   10

Respecting Others: Do you use others sexually for your selfish gratification, manipulating, deceiving, and leading them on to get what you want?

1   2   3   4   5   6   7   8   9   10

But among you there must not be even a hint of sexual immorality, or of any kind of impurity, or of greed, because these are improper for God's holy people.
Ephesians 5:3

<u>Purity in Thoughts:</u>

1   2   3   4   5   6   7   8   9   10

May the words of my mouth and the meditation of my heart be pleasing in your sight, O Lord, my Rock and my Redeemer.
Psalm 19:14 (NIV 1984)

THOUGHT LIFE: How is your thought life? Is it plagued with greed, pride, lust, fantasy, destructive thoughts, passivity, evil, hatred, murder, filth, jealousy, doubt, regret, fear, dread, or thoughts you just can't control?

1   2   3   4   5   6   7   8   9   10

IN GENERAL, HOW WOULD YOU RATE YOUR CHARACTER?

1   2   3   4   5   6   7   8   9   10

Take Heart!

At this point, you may feel like giving up, saying, "It's impossible. Why even bother?" Taking a look at our inner core can be eye-opening and discouraging. Think about this:

God did not send us His Holy Spirit—the Helper, Counselor, Advocate (Lawyer)—to do easy things we can do on our own. He sent us His Holy Spirit to do what we cannot do for ourselves. If you're feeling helpless, you are right on track. God cannot work on behalf of those who think they are "pretty good," "not as bad as," "not so bad," or "could be worse." And the bottom line is this: everyone begins with a mess, whether they want to admit it or not. Isaiah 64:6 says,

All of us have become like one who is unclean, and all our righteous acts are like filthy rags; we all shrivel up like a leaf, and like the wind our sins sweep us away.

That is precisely why we are in desperate need of a Savior. So, if today you find yourself a "big mess" and are willing to face up to it, congratulations! You've crossed the first hurdle.

SOUL SEARCH AND RATE YOURSELF THE PAST SIX MONTHS
DAY 10: *Are you a good steward of what God has entrusted to you?*

Go to the Baseline Data Table on DAY 30 and rate yourself.

DAY 11
WALKING IN TRUTH

Then you will know the truth, and the truth will set you free.
John 8:32

* * *

Are you walking in "the truth?"
To walk in "the truth" one must:

1. Know "the truth." ***"To the Jews who had believed him, Jesus said, 'If you hold to my teaching, you are really my disciples. Then you will know the truth, and the truth will set you free.'"*** (John 8:31-32)
Before you can walk in "the truth" you have to learn what it is and what it is not. Many people claim to have found "the truth." However, as believers, we find truth from only one source: the Word of God—the Bible. To learn "the truth," one must study the precepts of God's Word and then obey them.
2. Choose "the truth." ***"I have chosen the way of truth; I have set my heart on your laws."*** (Psalm 119:30, NIV 1984)
Have you chosen truth?

Walking Out the Truth

Do your best to present yourself to God as one approved, a worker who does not need to be ashamed and who correctly handles the word of truth.
2 Timothy 2:15

Walking out "the truth" is living the truth of God's Word in your day-to-day experience. Are you a person of truth, as demonstrated by your actions? Walking out "the truth" is not just speaking "the truth." It also includes acting in accordance with truth. If we attempt to make our lives appear to be something they are not, we are not walking out "the truth."

The Lord abhors dishonest scales, but accurate weights are his delight.
Proverbs 11:1 (NIV 1984)

In ancient days, scales were used to measure gold, silver, etc. A stone was used as the standard. Unscrupulous business men would mark their stones with a dishonest measurement.
In what ways are you deceiving others?

- Not being completely honest on taxes
- Telling a "little white lie"
- Giving a compliment you don't mean
- Not paying bills on time or not paying them at all
- Bouncing a check or having an overdraft
- Using your grandmother's handicap permit to park close to the storefront, even though your grandma isn't in the car with you
- Making an excuse for not doing something someone has asked you to do instead of just saying "No, thank you" or "I'm not interested"
- Covering for someone
- Breaking your promise of faithfulness to your spouse in word, thought, or deed
- Being dishonest about the time you spend on the job
- Doing personal errands on the clock
- Spending time on the Internet when you are supposed to be working

- Reporting too many miles
- Telling people what they want to hear

Challenge #11

Do you have any "dishonest scales" situations in your life—areas in which you are not living the way you say you believe?
_____
_____
_____

SOUL SEARCH AND RATE YOURSELF THE PAST SIX MONTHS
DAY 11: Are you walking in truth?

Go to the Baseline Data Table on DAY 30 and rate yourself.

DAY 12
IS YOUR WORD YOUR BOND?

It is better not to make a vow than to make one and not fulfill it.
Ecclesiastes 5:5

* * *

A half century ago, this principle was part of the American culture. It's sad that we have shifted from being people of our word to people of convenience. Talk is cheap and the days of people sticking to their promises and commitments seem to be long gone.

Do promises flow from your lips with little if any follow-through? Take a look at what Psalm 15 says about keeping your oath/promise:

Lord, who may dwell in your sacred tent? Who may live on your holy mountain? The one whose walk is blameless, who does what is righteous, who speaks the truth from their heart; whose tongue utters no slander, who does no wrong to a neighbor, and casts no slur on others; who despises a vile person but honors those who fear the Lord, who keeps an oath even when it hurts, and does not change their mind; who lends money to the poor without interest; who does not accept a bribe against the innocent. Whoever does these things will never be shaken.

Keeping your word is a big deal to God. His Word is His bond and He watches over it to perform it (Jeremiah 1:12, Amplified Bible). We are told in Hebrews 6:18 that it is impossible for Him to lie.

Challenge #12

Examine the words that have proceeded out of your mouth regarding promises and commitments, as well as commitments you have made via contracts and agreements. Use the following to help jog your memory. Have you promised to do any of the following, but haven't gotten around to it?

- Take your kids/family somewhere or do something with them
- Pay someone for a service, product, etc.
- Break a habit/start a habit
- Wake up early to pray, read your Bible, etc.
- Return phone calls
- Tell friends or acquaintances, "Let's do lunch," but fail to follow through
- Volunteer for a project

Many times, this is a sin of omission rather than commission, and we need to do a better job of writing down commitments or remembering what we have agreed to do. In many cases, we just forget. It's not that we don't intend to follow through. We just get busy with life. I know, because I am guilty of this and am committed to doing a better job.

How about you? Is your word your bond? Do people know that when you make an agreement they can bank on it, or is there little expectation that you will deliver? Is your talk cheap?

_____
_____
_____
_____
_____
_____

SOUL SEARCH AND RATE YOURSELF THE PAST SIX MONTHS
DAY 12: Is your word your bond?

Go to the Baseline Data Table on DAY 30 and rate yourself.

DAY 13
SELF-CONTROL

Like a city whose walls are broken through is a person who lacks self-control.
Proverbs 25:28

* * *

In ancient times, when this verse was written, cities were built with walls around them. The walls served as a defense. If a city's walls were broken down, not only was the city defenseless, it was disgraced as well. So too is anyone without self-control.

A person lacking self-control is defenseless to temptation. He is a slave to his impulses and thoughts. In addition to making us defenseless, self-control also brings disgrace. Being a slave to anyone or anything, other than Christ, always has this effect. Think a moment about people you know who are out of control in an area of their life. What is the effect? Honor and dignity or shame and disgrace?

The paradox of being a slave to Christ and righteousness is that it is the only way to freedom and peace. Romans 6:16 says,

Don't you know that when you offer yourselves to someone as obedient slaves, you are slaves of the one you obey—whether you are slaves to sin, which leads to death, or to obedience, which leads to righteousness?

How exactly do we acquire self-control? Consider the following four ways:

    1.) Self-control is acquired by natural tendency. We all know someone who seems like the consummate drill sergeant. It's in her DNA. She is just naturally predisposed to being self-controlled. These people aren't off the hook when it comes to pursuing self-control. However, they will have an easier time in their quest, as it's part of their makeup and they highly value this quality. You either have it or you don't. If you don't possess this trait naturally, you are not exempt from acquiring it. Rather, you will have to work all the harder to obtain it.

2.) Self-Control is acquired by family environment. If you grow up in a structured family that not only values self-control but requires it, you likely will have this trait to some degree, even though it may not be a natural tendency for you. This is where parents have an awesome opportunity to instill a quality that will determine their child's success or failure. If you're a parent, don't pass up this opportunity! The pain of learning this lesson is much less when we're under eighteen than it is when we're adults. Save your children the heartache. Have them pay up front. They (and you) will enjoy the benefits for the rest of their lives.

3.) Self-control is acquired by remaining in Christ. This simply means yielding your life to Christ and spending time in His Word (the Bible) and prayer. The key is remaining, which implies consistency. It implies doing it continually. In Galatians 5:23, the Bible refers to self-control as the fruit of the Spirit. Self-control is produced when we remain in Christ. Take a look at John 15:5: ***"I am the vine; you are the branches. If you remain in me and I in you, you will bear much fruit; apart from me you can do nothing."***

Have you been trying to bear fruit apart from Christ? If so, your efforts are in vain. However, if you remain in Christ, you'll produce fruit. You may not see it right away, but don't be discouraged. An apple tree doesn't bear apples 365 days a year. It bears apples in fall. The same applies to you. Psalm 1:1-3 tells us that when we delight in God's Word and spend time reading it, meditating on it, and obeying it, we are like a tree that bears fruit "in its season." So be encouraged. If you are remaining in Christ, yet not seeing results, it's just not yet harvest time.

4.) Self-Control is acquired by making a choice. If you desire to be a person of self-control, you will have to make the choice and then do the hard work that goes along with it. We see from God's Word we are to be self-controlled. In other words, regulate yourself. This is your responsibility, something you must do. Because God would never tell us to do something we are unable to do, it also implies that we can do this. Study the following scriptures:

So then, let us not be like others, who are asleep, but let us be alert and self-controlled. (1 Thessalonians 5:6, NIV 1984)

But since we belong to the day, let us be self-controlled. (I Thessalonians 5:8a, NIV 1984)

Teach the older men to be . . . self-controlled. (Titus 2:2a)

... Train the younger women . . . to be self-controlled. (Titus 2:4-5a, NIV 1984)

> ***Similarly, encourage the young men to be self-controlled.*** (Titus 2:6)
>
> ***Therefore, prepare your minds for action; be self-controlled.*** (1 Peter 1:13a, NIV 1984)
>
> ***Be clear minded and self-controlled so that you can pray.*** (1 Peter 4:7b, NIV 1984)
>
> ***Be self-controlled and alert.*** (1 Peter 5:8a, NIV 1984)
>
> ***... Make every effort to add . . . self-control.*** (2 Peter 1:5-6)
>
> ***For the grace of God has appeared that offers salvation to all people. It teaches us to say "No" to ungodliness and worldly passions, and to live self-controlled, upright and godly lives in this present age.*** (Titus 2:11-12)

You obviously don't have a say in the first two methods of obtaining self-control. However, your choice to be self-controlled rests solely on you. Ultimately, the buck stops with you. You are responsible for your self-control or lack of it. We are told in 2 Timothy 1:7 that God has given us a spirit of self-control. You are not a helpless victim of your impulses and desires. You have the power of choice, along with the power of God to help you take control of your life. The choice is up to you.

Challenge #13

On a scale from 1-5, rate your level of self-control in the following areas:

_____ Self-Control as a Natural Tendency
_____ Self-Control as a Result of Family Environment
_____ Self-Control as a Result of Remaining in Christ
_____ Self-Control as a Result of Choice

Because self-control is such a broad area, we will break it down into smaller parts: thoughts, words, and actions.

SOUL SEARCH AND RATE YOURSELF THE PAST SIX MONTHS
DAY 13: Using the analogy of the city with walls, how strong are your walls when it comes to self-control?

Go to the Baseline Data Table on DAY 30 and rate yourself.

DAY 14
SELF-CONTROL: THOUGHTS

Finally, brothers and sisters, whatever is true, whatever is noble, whatever is right, whatever is pure, whatever is lovely, whatever is admirable—if anything is excellent or praiseworthy—think about such things.
Philippians 4:8

* * *

What are you thinking about? What kinds of thoughts fill your mind throughout the day? Pure, noble, and positive thoughts or:
- Impure thoughts
- Daydreaming and fantasizing
- Worry, dread, fear, or regret
- Tormenting thoughts
- Ways to gratify your desires
- "Me, Myself, and I"

The Bible gives a clear picture of what the mind of a self-controlled person looks like. Are your thoughts true, noble, right, pure, lovely, admirable, excellent, and praiseworthy? These are all traits of a self-controlled mind.

Another trait of a self-controlled mind is action. Some Christians have the notion that the life of a Christian is a passive, go-with-the-flow existence. They spend their time talking about "walking in the Spirit" but never really follow through on their actions. For them, "walking in the Spirit" is a license to be a spiritual flake, void of all thinking and common sense.

Matthew 22:37 says that we are to love God with all our heart, soul, and mind. God could have stopped after the heart and soul, but He didn't. He wants us to use our minds for His glory. Still not convinced? Take a look at the following verses. Some of them will be familiar from the previous section.

> ***So then, let us not be like others, who are asleep, but let us be alert and self-controlled.***
> 1 Thessalonians 5:6 (NIV 1984)

> ***Be on guard! Be alert! You do not know when that time will come.***
> Mark 13:33

> ***Be alert and always keep on praying for all the Lord's people.***
> Ephesians 6:18b

> ***Be self-controlled and alert. Your enemy the devil prowls around like a roaring lion looking for someone to devour.***
> 1 Peter 5:8 (NIV 1984)

    As we can see from these scriptures, we are to be alert. An alert mind is anything but passive. An alert mind is on the offensive, prepared and ready. It gives us a picture of a soldier who has been trained, is highly skilled, ready for combat, and prepared for action. Is that a picture of your mind or are you overtaken by every impulsive thought and urge that comes your way?

    One of my favorite quotes comes from Andrew Carnegie, who said, "The man who acquires the ability to take full possession of his own mind may take possession of anything else to which he is justly entitled."

    It all begins here. Have you taken full possession of your mind? I like to call this "conquering yourself" or "mastering yourself." It's a greater feat than winning the ultimate esteemed prize in any sport, reaching the pinnacle of success in your field of work, being elected to the highest office in the land, or acquiring fame and fortune.

How is this achieved? By gaining control of your mind.

Your mind is like a vacuum. It's going to be filled with something. The beauty is that you get to choose what that "something" is. How would you like that "something" to be "perfect peace?" Who wouldn't choose a peaceful mind over a tormenting, badgering, unruly, and impulsive mind? Isaiah 26:3 outlines the steps to perfect peace:

You will keep in perfect peace those whose minds are steadfast, because they trust in you.

The qualifier for perfect peace is a steadfast mind. How does one attain a steadfast mind? Psalm 1:1-3 outlines the process:

Blessed is the one who does not walk in step with the wicked or stand in the way that sinners take or sit in the company of mockers, but whose delight is in the law of the Lord, and who meditates on his law day and night. That person is like a tree planted by streams of water, which yields its fruit in season and whose leaf does not wither—whatever they do prospers.

This psalm gives a beautiful picture of a steadfast mind. This is an individual who is not casual about God's Word. Rather, this individual loves God's Word so much that she delights in it, and this makes her think about it constantly. She ponders its principles and application for her life. In essence, she is filling her mind with God's Word.

Challenge # 14

Getting control of one's mind may be the most difficult part of *The 30-Day Character Challenge.* If you are in the habit of letting your mind wander wherever it pleases, be prepared for the work ahead. You didn't get your mind into the mess it's in overnight, and you won't get your mind out of the mess overnight. Progress may be slow and from time to time you may encounter setbacks. Just don't stop.

Take a look at the mind of the Spirit and the mind of the flesh. Which one describes you? Circle the adjectives that describe your character.

Mind of the Spirit	**Mind of the Flesh**
Love	Depraved
Joy	Greed
Peace	Evil thoughts
Patience	Envy
Kindness	Unsubmissive to God
Goodness	Focused on earthy things
Faithfulness	Hatred
Gentleness	Fantasy and Daydreaming
Self-Control	Fear
Renewed	Depression
Meditating on God's Word	Doubt, Worry, Regret, Dread
Humility	Lust
Alert	Selfishness
Obedient to God	Pride
Focused on God	Torment
Assurance	Impatience

Does your mind fall into the category of the Mind of the Spirit or the Mind of the Flesh? If you answered the latter, you have your work cut out for you. God's ready to help if you will do your part.

Romans 12:2 tells us that our lives will be transformed when we renew our minds:

Do not conform to the pattern of this world, but be transformed by the renewing of your mind. Then you will be able to test and approve what God's will is—his good, pleasing and perfect will.

Renewing your mind simply means replacing your thoughts with God's thoughts (found by reading God's Word). Begin the renewal process today by taking the following steps:

1.) Daily spend time reading God's Word. If this is new to you, and you don't know where to start, begin reading the gospels: Matthew, Mark, Luke, and John. Start by reading part of or an entire chapter a day. Sometimes you may read only a few verses before one verse jumps out at you. That may be your cue that you are to stop and let God speak to you about that particular thought. Psalms and Proverbs are easy, encouraging reads that you may also want to include in your Bible study.
2.) Don't stop at reading God's Word. Meditate on it (Joshua 1:8). Meditating means to say it over and over, thinking about how it applies to you as well as how you can apply it to your life.
3.) Pray. Ask God to reveal His Word to you. Also ask Him for help in renewing your mind.
4.) Journal. Write down verses that speak to you. Turn those verses into a prayer back to God.

SOUL SEARCH AND RATE YOURSELF THE PAST SIX MONTHS
DAY 14: How would you rate self-control in your thought life?

Go to the Baseline Data Table on DAY 30 and rate yourself.

DAY 15
SELF-CONTROL: WORDS

For the mouth speaks what the heart is full of.
Matthew 12:34b

* * *

It is fascinating that we can be in someone's presence for a short period of time and get a good picture of the kind of person he is. Our words reveal our core. On a regular basis, politicians and celebrities make comments that are appalling and despicable. Reacting to public backlash, these individuals make a public statement, something to the effect that they are sorry if their comments offended anyone. What they should say is, "Yes, you heard it right. I meant every word I said."

The same is true for us. When unkind, destructive, and hurtful words come out of our mouth, it's easy to say, "I'm sorry. I didn't mean it." Actually, yes, we did mean it. Our words just revealed what was hidden in our heart. I say "hidden" because we may not have known what was in our heart, and it may come as a surprise even to us.

In these situations an apology is necessary. However, we need to stop saying, "I didn't mean it." Rather, we need to understand that our words indicate what's stored up inside. They are a symptom of a deeper problem. If we change what's inside our heart, our words will follow suit.

How do we do this? By cooperating with God as he works on our deepest parts. And we cooperate with God by changing our thoughts to His thoughts regarding people and situations, as well as asking for His help. It's also beneficial to spend time with people who will contribute to our quest of speaking constructive, kind, and wholesome words.

What do your words reveal about your heart? As you take today's challenge, keep Matthew 12:34, our verse at the beginning of this chapter, front and center.

CHALLENGE #15

Answer the following 27 questions. Give yourself a "1" if you can answer "yes" to the first half of the question. If your answer is "no" to the first half of the question, give yourself a "0."

1.) Do your words bring healing **OR** do they pierce like a sword?

> ***The words of the reckless pierce like swords, but the tongue of the wise brings healing.*** (Proverbs 12:18)

2.) Do you guard your lips **OR** do you speak rashly (without thought of what you are saying)?

> ***Those who guard their lips preserve their lives, but those who speak rashly will come to ruin.*** (Proverbs 13:3)

> ***Those who consider themselves religious and yet do not keep a tight rein on their tongues deceive themselves, and their religion is worthless.*** (James 1:26)

> ***Those who guard their mouths and their tongues keep themselves from calamity.*** (Proverbs 21:23)

3.) Do you speak pleasant **OR** unpleasant words?

> ***Gracious words are a honeycomb, sweet to the soul and healing to the bones.*** (Proverbs 16:24)

4.) Do you use words with restraint **OR** do they flow freely from your lips without much thought?

> ***The one who has knowledge uses words with restraint, and whoever has understanding is even-tempered.*** (Proverbs 17:27)

5.) Is your speech gracious **OR** is it rude and unbecoming?

> ***Let your conversation be always full of grace, seasoned with salt, so that you may know how to answer everyone.*** (Colossians 4:6)

> ***Words from the mouth of the wise are gracious, but fools are consumed by their own lips.*** (Ecclesiastes 10:12)

6.) What comes out of your mouth, good things OR evil things?

> ***A good man brings good things out of the good stored up in him, and an evil man brings evil things out of the evil stored up in him.*** (Matthew 12:35)

7.) Is your speech beneficial in building others up **OR** does it tear down?

> ***Do not let any unwholesome talk come out of your mouths, but only what is helpful for building others up according to their needs,***

> *that it may benefit those who listen.* (Ephesians 4:29)

8.) Are your words pleasing to God **OR** do they grieve His heart?

> *May the words of my mouth and the meditation of my heart be pleasing in your sight, O Lord, my Rock and my Redeemer.* (Psalm 19:14, NIV 1984)

9.) Are the words of your mouth pure **OR** are they unwholesome and corrupt?

> *Keep your mouth free of perversity; keep corrupt talk far from your lips.* (Proverbs 4:24)

10.) Do you hold your tongue **OR** talk all the time?

> *When words are many, sin is not absent, but he who holds his tongue is wise.* (Proverbs 10:19, NIV 1984)

11.) Do you speak the truth in love **OR** do you tell people what they want to hear?

> *Whoever rebukes a person will in the end gain favor rather than one who has a flattering tongue.* (Proverbs 28:23)

12.) Do you speak the truth **OR** do you have lying lips?

> *The Lord detests lying lips, but he delights in people who are trustworthy.* (Proverbs 12:22)

> ***Do not lie to each other, since you have taken off your old self with its practices.*** (Colossians 3:9)

> ***There are six things the Lord hates, seven that are detestable to him: . . . a lying tongue . . . a false witness who pours out lies.*** (Proverbs 6:16, 17, 19a)

13.) Do you speak kindly of others **OR** do you use your tongue to gossip?

> ***A gossip betrays a confidence; so avoid anyone who talks too much.*** (Proverbs 20:19)

14.) Can you keep a secret **OR** do you betray another's confidence?

> ***A gossip betrays a confidence, but a trustworthy person keeps a secret.*** (Proverbs 11:13)

15.) Do you keep your knowledge to yourself **OR** are you a know-it-all, constantly telling people what you "know" or what you "think"?

> ***The prudent keep their knowledge to themselves, but a fool's heart blurts out folly.*** (Proverbs 12:23)

16.) Are you humble and keep your accomplishments to yourself **OR** do you brag about yourself?

> ***Let someone else praise you, and not your own mouth; an outsider, and not your own lips.*** (Proverbs 27:2)

17.) Do your lips give a clear and accurate picture of reality **OR** do you use them to misrepresent the truth and deceive people into believing things that are not true and 100 percent accurate?

> . . . *"Whoever would love life and see good days must keep their tongue from evil and their lips from deceitful speech."* (1 Peter 3:10)
>
> *Differing weights and differing measures—the Lord detests them both.* (Proverbs 20:10)
>
> *The Lord detests differing weights, and dishonest scales do not please him.* (Proverbs 20:23)

18.) Do you speak gracious of others **OR** is your speech malicious and slanderous?

> *One who loves a pure heart and who speaks with grace will have the king for a friend.* (Proverbs 22:11)
>
> *But now you must also rid yourselves of all such things as these: anger, rage, malice, slander, and filthy language from your lips.* (Colossians 3:8)
>
> *Remind the people to . . . slander no one.* (Titus 3:1-2a)

19.) Is your speech pure, fitting, and appropriate **OR** is your speech perverse and inappropriate?

> *The thoughts of the wicked are shamefully vile and exceedingly offensive to the Lord, but the words of the pure are pleasing words to Him.* (Proverbs 15:26, AMP)

> *The lips of the righteous know what is fitting, but the mouth of the wicked only what is perverse.* (Proverbs 10:32, NIV 1984)

20.) Do you under-commit and over-deliver **OR** do you over-commit and under-deliver? Do you keep your promises and commitments, even the small ones that flow quickly out of your mouth, such as, "I'll give you a call"?

> *It is a trap to dedicate something rashly and only later to consider one's vows.* (Proverbs 20:25)

> *I will fulfill my vows to the Lord in the presence of all his people.* (Psalm 116:14)

> *When a man makes a vow to the Lord or takes an oath to obligate himself by a pledge, he must not break his word but must do everything he said.* (Numbers 30:2)

21.) Are God's words continually in your mouth **OR** is it a rare occasion that God's Word is found in your mouth?

> *This Book of the Law shall not depart out of your mouth, but you shall meditate on it day and night, that you may observe and do according to all that is written in it. For then you shall make your way prosperous, and then you shall deal wisely and have good success.* (Joshua 1:8, AMP)

22.) Are God's praises continually on your lips **OR** is praise the furthest thing from your lips?

> *My tongue will proclaim your righteousness, your praises all day long.* (Psalm 35:28)

23.) Are you purposely using your mouth to be a blessing to others **OR** are you passing up opportunities to speak good?

> *[The Servant of God says] The Lord God has given Me the tongue of a disciple and of one who is taught, that I should know how to speak a word in season to him who is weary. He wakens Me morning by morning, He wakens My ear to hear as a disciple [as one who is taught].* (Isaiah 50:4, AMP)

> *Do not withhold good from those to whom it is due, when it is in your power to act.* (Proverbs 3:27)

24.) Are you grateful **OR** a complainer?

> *Do everything without complaining or arguing.* (Philippians 2:14, NIV 1984)

25.) Do you cease from strife **OR** do you argue and quarrel?

> *It is to one's honor to avoid strife, but every fool is quick to quarrel.* (Proverbs 20:3)

> *Whoever loves a quarrel loves sin; whoever builds a high gate invites destruction.* (Proverbs 17:19)

26.) Do you repay evil and insults with blessing **OR** do you repay evil with evil and insult with insult?

> ***Do not repay evil with evil or insult with insult. On the contrary, repay evil with blessing, because to this you were called so that you may inherit a blessing.*** (1 Peter 3:9)

27.) Do you listen to both sides before you give your opinion **OR** do you give your opinion before you hear the facts?

> ***To answer before listening—that is folly and shame.*** (Proverbs 18:13)

Record your results from the previous questions in the following table.

SELF-CONTROLLED TONGUE Give Yourself a "1"	SCORE	UNCONTROLLED TONGUE Give Yourself a "0"
Careful what you say		Reckless words
Guard your lips		Speak rashly, without thought to what you are saying
Speak pleasant words		Speak unpleasant words
Use words with restraint		Words flow freely with no thought of what you say
Gracious speech		Rude and unbecoming speech
Speak good things		Speak evil things

SELF-CONTROLLED TONGUE Give Yourself a "1"	SCORE	UNCONTROLLED TONGUE Give Yourself a "0"
Speech beneficial in building others up		Tear down others
Pleasing to God		Displeasing to God
Pure		Unwholesome, perverse, corrupt speech
Hold your tongue		Talk continuously
Speak the truth in love		Say what others want to hear
Tell the truth		Speak lies
Speak kindly of others		Gossip
Keep a secret		Betray a confidence
Keep your knowledge to yourself		Know-it-all
Humble		Brag
Give an accurate picture, description, account		Misrepresent the facts, deceive by exaggerating, leave out important facts
Speak gracious of others		Malicious and slanderous
Pure, fitting, and appropriate		Crude, filthy, inappropriate talk
Under-commit and over-deliver		Over-commit and under-deliver
God's words are found in your mouth		God's words absent from your mouth

SELF-CONTROLLED TONGUE Give Yourself a "1"	SCORE	UNCONTROLLED TONGUE Give Yourself a "0"
God's praises are on your lips		God's praises absent from your lips
Use opportunities to bless others with your mouth		Pass up opportunities to bless others with your mouth
Grateful		Complain
Refrain from arguing		Argue
Repay evil and insult with blessing		Repay evil with evil and insult with insult
Listen to both sides before you give your opinion		Speak before you know the facts
	Total Score = _____	

Score:
27-20: You have a good deal of self-control when it comes to your mouth.
19-12: You have some self-control of your mouth, but plenty of room for improvement.
11-0: You are in desperate need for self-control of your mouth.

Assess the condition of your mouth. Where are your weaknesses? Here are some steps to help you control your tongue:

1.) Ask for God's help
2.) Store up good things in your heart. (Recognize that what flows from your mouth starts in your heart.) To store up good things in your heart, begin reading God's Word, memorizing it, and meditating on it (speaking it over and over as you contemplate its meaning and significance in your life.)
3.) Make a choice and then use self-control to follow through!

SOUL SEARCH AND RATE YOURSELF THE PAST SIX MONTHS
DAY 15: How would you rate self-control with your tongue?

Go to the Baseline Data Table on DAY 30 and rate yourself.

DAY 16
SELF-CONTROL: ACTIONS

Moderation is better than muscle, self-control better than political power.
Proverbs 16:32 (The Message)

* * *

In the process of editing this study, I attended a wedding with my two daughters. During the ceremony, my 4-year-old, Sophie, began to get restless. I gently reminded her to sit still. After a couple of reminders, she whispered to me, "Mom, I told my body "No," but it disobeyed me."

Out of the mouths of babes! She beautifully described the struggle of learning self-control—a struggle we face all throughout our life.

As we stated earlier, self-control is part of the fruit of the Spirit (Galatians 5:22-23), which is produced by remaining in the vine, Jesus Christ (John 15:5). We have the responsibility to remain in Christ if we want to produce self-control.

Not only are we told to remain in Christ, we can also see from these scriptures that bearing fruit is the natural consequence of doing so. In the introduction to this book, I referred to 2 Peter chapter one as the character chapter of the Bible. Let's take a look at verses 3-9, which give us more instruction on our role in producing the fruit of self-control.

His divine power has given us everything we need for a godly life through our knowledge of him who called us by his own glory and goodness. Through these he has given us his very great and precious promises, so that through them you may participate in the divine nature, having escaped the corruption

in the world caused by evil desires. For this very reason, make every effort to add to your faith goodness; and to goodness, knowledge; and to knowledge, self-control; and to self-control, perseverance; and to perseverance, godliness; and to godliness, mutual affection; and to mutual affection, love. For if you possess these qualities in increasing measure, they will keep you from being ineffective and unproductive in your knowledge of our Lord Jesus Christ. But whoever does not have them is nearsighted and blind, forgetting that they have been cleansed from their past sins.

From these scriptures we can gain the following insight:
1.) God has given us everything we need for godliness. Your quest for self-control is not impossible. If you pursue it His way, you can have it.
2.) This godliness comes through knowledge that Christ wants to make known to you. It's not some great mystery or secret that He is keeping from you. The more you know about God, His ways, His thoughts, and His principles, the greater is your capacity to bear fruit. Please note: knowledge by itself won't bear fruit, but knowledge with obedience will.
3.) Through God's promises (His Word and obedience to His Word), we can escape from evil desires. In essence, this is self-control.
4.) We are told that we are to make every effort to add self-control. (We will focus on this in just a moment.)
5.) We are to possess self-control (along with the other characteristics mentioned) in increasing measure. We need to acquire greater degrees of self-control continually.

6.) If you possess self-control (and the other characteristics) in increasing measure, you will be effective and productive. Failure to do so results in being "nearsighted and blind."

Let's take a closer look at point #4: adding self-control. Are you doing everything you can to add self-control to your life? I like to call this setting yourself up for success. Ask yourself the following questions and find out whether you are setting yourself up for success.

Question 1:
Have you created an environment that is conducive to living a self-controlled life and non-conducive to living without self-control? Galatians 5:16 explains it this way:

So I say, walk by the Spirit, and you will not gratify the desires of the flesh.

For example, if you struggle with:

- alcohol or drugs, do you take the necessary measures to eliminate temptation? Do you avoid the very scenes of temptation?
- overeating, have you set up your environment so you have eliminated or greatly reduced those foods and situations that pose the greatest challenge?
- pornography, do you have safeguards on your computer? Have you cancelled your cable subscription to channels that offer that kind of programming? Do you hold yourself accountable to someone such as your spouse and allow them access to your internet viewing?

Not all situations of self-control are created equal. Some require a clean break. For example, if you struggle with alcohol, eliminate it completely. This may sound extreme, but how serious are you about walking in self-control and being a person of character? If you are telling yourself you can handle it, even though you've had issues with it in the past, you are deceiving yourself.

On the other hand, in situations like overeating, a clean break is not possible. Obviously, you can't eliminate eating altogether, but you can eliminate having unhealthy food and snacks as well as tempting food in your house, car, purse, locker, and desk. You can stop going to the restaurants that present temptation to you. If your greatest source of temptation is the grocery store, send a family member to do the grocery shopping for you. You may not have to do this permanently, but it may be what you need initially to form new habits.

If you struggle with gossip, you obviously can't stop talking altogether, but you can eliminate the scenes in which you find yourself engaging in this kind of activity. Is it during the lunch hour? Quit eating lunch with those individuals you gossip with and start walking or exercising. Is it at the salon? Find a new one. Is it at certain events such as parties, Bible studies, or girls' night out? Either shut down the talk or stop attending.

> ***If your hand or your foot causes you to stumble, cut it off and throw it away. It is better for you to enter life maimed or crippled than to have two hands or two feet and be thrown into eternal fire.***
> Matthew 18:8

Question 2:
Have you established relationships that are conducive to a self-controlled life? More specifically, how self-controlled

are the people you spend the majority of your time with? You become like the people with whom you socialize.

> ***As iron sharpens iron, so one person sharpens another.***
> Proverbs 27:17

Do your friends sharpen your tendency to be self-controlled, or do they sharpen your tendency to be out of control and impulsive?

Question 3:
Do you think ahead and then make plans to avoid tempting situations? Or are you constantly blindsided because you are not prepared for inevitable temptation?

> ***The prudent see danger and take refuge, but the simple keep going and pay the penalty.***
> Proverbs 22:3

Question 4:
Do you put yourself in compromising situations because you think you can handle it? Do you think the little things don't matter? These "little things" can be compared to the "little foxes" of Song of Songs:

> ***Catch for us the foxes, the little foxes that ruin the vineyards, our vineyards that are in bloom.***
> Song of Songs 2:15

For example, "I know I have a problem with …

- shopping, but just going to the store and looking never hurt anyone."
- cheesecake, but just a little bite won't hurt."
- gambling, but I'll only spend twenty dollars."

- lust, but I promise to turn off TV if I start to feel tempted."
- gossiping and speaking maliciously around that group of friends, but I won't join in on their conversation."
- stealing, but I can handle getting a job in which I'm constantly around other people's money."
- fantasizing and daydreaming, but reading this romance novel or watching a soap opera is relaxing, and I can control my thoughts."
- sexual desire, but a little kissing and making out won't hurt."

We are told in Philippians 3:3 that we should put no confidence in the flesh. Your flesh (that part of you that acts independently of God) cannot be trusted, ever!

Do you want to walk in self-control and significantly decrease the temptations that plague your soul? 1 Corinthians 10:13 (The Message) says,

No test or temptation that comes your way is beyond the course of what others have had to face. All you need to remember is that God will never let you down; he'll never let you be pushed past your limit; he'll always be there to help you come through it.

Often, God's way out is for you to "get out" as quickly as you can. Another word for a way out or getting out is "abstinence." In 1 Peter 2:11, we are exhorted,

Dear friends, I urge you, as foreigners and exiles, to abstain from sinful desires, which wage war against your soul.

Do not deceive yourself into thinking you have everything under control and can handle it. If you violate the principle of not letting in the "little foxes" (compromise), your flesh will take you over the edge, every single time. Slam the door. Don't let the "little foxes" in.

Question 5:
Do you understand and use the home-court advantage? My husband is a graduate of both Kansas State University and Kansas University. As a huge fan of the K-State Wildcats, he keeps close dibs on their football and basketball teams. Once he told me that the Big 12 men's basketball teams had a 114-1 record on their home court against out-of-conference opponents for the season. hat is an incredible winning record of 99 percent. And it's not an isolated phenomenon. Anyone involved in athletics knows the advantage of playing on their own turf.

The same holds true when it comes to us and temptation. Take a look at James 1:14. It tells us how we are tempted:

But each person is tempted when they are dragged away by their own evil desire and enticed.

We can see from this scripture that we are dragged away in temptation. Dragged away from where? From our "home court."

As a Christian, your "home court" is being plugged into God through meditating on His Word, obeying His Word, delighting in His Word and prayer, and being around other believers who are walking out God's commands. When you unplug from God and these activities, you allow yourself to be dragged away to the court of your opponent, the devil. Want to know another amazing home-court statistic? The devil's home court record is 100 percent. He wins "at home" every time. You are no match to his deceptive schemes.

With those kinds of statistics, it only makes sense to keep the home-court advantage. Unlike a sports competition, when it comes to shielding yourself from temptation, you can have the home-court advantage every time if you choose. King David understood this as he wrote,

> ***I have hidden your word in my heart that I might not sin against you.***
> Psalm 119:11

CHALLENGE #16

1.) Let's Recap. Answer the following questions.

    A.) Have you created an environment conducive to living a self-controlled life?
___

    B.) Have you established relationships conducive to living a self-controlled life?
___

    C.) Do you think ahead and then make plans to avoid tempting situations, or are you constantly blindsided because you are not prepared for inevitable temptation?
___

    D.) Do you put yourself in compromising situations because you think you can handle it?
___

    E.) Do you understand and utilize the home-court advantage?
___

2.) What trips you up and entangles you?
___
___
___

    Hebrews 12:1 tells us to throw off everything that hinders and the sin that so easily entangles. How can you stay between the lines with your particular self-control challenges?

This will look different for each of us. You know yourself better than anyone else does. If you're not quite sure, become a student of your behavior. Study those moments of greatest weakness and temptation, as well as your greatest strengths and victories. Include time of day, location, who you are with, time of year, your emotional state (happy, bored, sad, depressed), and other factors, such as influence of television, music, advertisements, etc.

Here's an Example:
Self-control challenge: overeating

<u>Moments of Vulnerability</u>
- Bored
- Lonely
- 3 p.m. while watching the Food Network
- Holidays
- Family get-togethers

<u>Staying Between the Lines—My Boundaries</u>
- When bored or lonely, call a friend for a walk or encouragement
- Schedule my workout (or some other activity) at 3 p.m.
- Have a plan for holidays with family get-togethers that include eating some of my favorite dishes and deserts

Now you give it a try:
Self-control challenge: _____

<u>Moments of Vulnerability</u>
- _____
- _____
- _____
- _____
- _____

Staying Between the Lines—My Boundaries

- _____
- _____
- _____
- _____
- _____

SOUL SEARCH AND RATE YOURSELF THE PAST SIX MONTHS
DAY 16: How would you rate self-control in your actions?

Go to the Baseline Data Table on DAY 30 and rate yourself.

DAY 17
OBEDIENCE OUT OF A PURE HEART

... This is love for God: to keep his commands. And his commands are not burdensome.
1 John 5:3

* * *

Do you love God? If you answer "yes" to that question, what do you base your answer on? If it's anything less than obedience to God, you have fooled yourself. The Bible tells us there is one key factor present in love for God, and that is obedience.

At this point, I know there are probably some who would say, "Now, hold on. I attend church, tithe, am a deacon, choir director/music leader, or Sunday school teacher. I give to the poor, and I feel love and reverence for God in my heart. Besides, I'm doing this Bible study!"

But do you obey God in every area of your life? I'm not talking about never making a mistake or slipping up from time to time. What I'm referring to is submitting control of your entire life to Christ and endeavoring to obey His law. When you get to this level of obedience, nothing is off limits. You give God permission to meddle in all areas of your life. Then you can say, "I love God."

Take a look at the following scriptures:

Jesus replied, "Anyone who loves me will obey my teaching."
John 14:23a

If you hold to my teaching, you are really my disciples.
John 8:31b

Answer the following question honestly. When you look at the level of obedience in the past six months, can you say you love God?

YES   NO

If you answered "No," understand forgiveness awaits and you can begin a life of obedience from this moment on. Once again, help is just a prayer away. Ask God to teach you obedience. Jesus was our example and even He, a man who never sinned, had to learn obedience:

Although he was a son, he learned obedience from what he suffered.
Hebrews 5:8 (NIV 1984)

If Jesus needed to learn obedience, how much more do we need to learn obedience? Psalm 119:33-34 (NIV 1984) gives us a prayer we can use to ask for God's help in learning and understanding his commands:

Teach me, O Lord, to follow your decrees; then I will keep them to the end. Give me understanding, and I will keep your law and obey it with all my heart.

Obedience with a Sincere Heart

Did you know you can obey God, but for all the wrong reasons? Many times, Christians obey God so they can get in on His blessings. They might tithe so God will bless them financially. Or maybe they give to the needy so people will see their generosity. They may deny themselves fattening and unhealthy foods in order to have a svelte body.)

God sees right through our motives and into the heart. He wants our obedience to be a product of the love we have for Him, not just as a means to get in on His blessings. If you're a parent, you can understand this. No one wants feigned obedience. Hebrews 10:22 says,

> **Let us draw near to God with a sincere heart and with the full assurance that faith brings, having our hearts sprinkled to cleanse us from a guilty conscience and having our bodies washed with pure water.**

King David is a good example of a heart that obeys God out of sincerity and a deep love for God. Psalm 63:1-8 (NIV 1984), is one of many indicators showing us why God called David a man after His own heart:

> *O God, you are my God, earnestly I seek you; my soul thirsts for you, my body longs for you, in a dry and weary land where there is no water.*
> *I have seen you in the sanctuary and beheld your power and your glory.*
> *Because your love is better than life, my lips will glorify you.*
> *I will praise you as long as I live, and in your name I will lift up my hands.*
> *My soul will be satisfied as with the richest of foods; with singing lips my mouth will praise you.*
> *On my bed I remember you; I think of you through the watches of the night.*
> *Because you are my help, I sing in the shadow of your wings.*
> *My soul clings to you; your right hand upholds me.*

Do you have this kind of love for God? Does your love result in sincere obedience?

Challenge #17

If you can't answer YES to the previous questions but wish you could, Psalm 51:10 offers a humble prayer you can make your own:

Create in me a pure heart, O God, and renew a steadfast spirit within me.

Do you need to repent (turn from your own ways) and turn to God? _____
Forgiveness waits:

Whoever conceals their sins does not prosper, but the one who confesses and renounces them finds mercy.
Proverbs 28:13

If we confess our sins, he is faithful and just and will forgive us our sins and purify us from all unrighteousness.
1 John 1:9

SOUL SEARCH AND RATE YOURSELF THE PAST SIX MONTHS
DAY 17: How would you rate the purity of your heart?

Go to the Baseline Data Table on DAY 30 and rate yourself.

DAY 18
APPROPRIATE BOUNDARY LINES

And he made from one man every nation of mankind to live on all the face of the earth, having determined allotted periods and the boundaries of their dwelling place.
Acts 17:26 (ESV)

* * *

Boundary lines represent your property lines. Everything that falls within those boundary lines is your responsibility. Everything outside them is none of your business. As adults, we set up our boundaries. It is our responsibility to discreetly determine the boundary lines in our thoughts, actions, words, relationships, commitments, and convictions.

With so many choices, how can we know what are appropriate boundaries? If you come from a background in which appropriate boundaries were the norm, this will be much easier for you. However, if you have never known boundaries, or at least not appropriate ones, you will have a lot to learn.

Fortunately, you are not alone. God's Word gives detailed instructions on boundaries. In some areas, we are told to abstain altogether. In others, we are told to live moderately. Let's take a further look at these two directives.

Abstaining

Dear friends, I urge you, as foreigners and exiles, to abstain from sinful desires, which wage war against your soul.
1 Peter 2:11

Anything God commands us to abstain from (such as sinful desires) falls outside our boundary lines. Our responsibility is to refrain from this kind of behavior. (Day 16 touches on this. You may want to refer back to Question 4.)

Moderation/Balance

Be well balanced (temperate, sober of mind), be vigilant and cautious at all times; for that enemy of yours, the devil, roams around like a lion roaring [in fierce hunger], seeking someone to seize upon and devour.
1 Peter 5:8 (AMP)

This is probably one of the believer's biggest challenges: living a moderate, temperate, balanced life. Many people love extremes: going all out one way or the other, being hard core. Consider the following extremes:

- Too much sleep **OR** lack of sleep
- Overworking **OR** laziness
- Gluttony **OR** starving oneself with extreme diets
- Gossiping/talking all the time **OR** not saying enough
- Wastefulness with money and time **OR** being selfish with one's resources
- Too much fun/pleasures **OR** not giving oneself license to enjoy life
- Too strict **OR** too lax as a parent
- Being harsh, mean, and unyielding with people **OR** allowing people to walk all over you and take advantage of you
- Over-commitment **OR** no commitments to people, organizations, church, school, or community

According to 1 Peter 5:8, we set ourselves up as targets for the enemy when we get out of balance. In these times, we are most vulnerable to his attacks. It's as if we are posting a bull's-eye on our back.

There are times in life when we experience a temporary imbalance, but this should not be the norm. Just as crossing the lines on the highway will eventually spell disaster, crossing the lines in your spiritual, personal, financial, professional, and social life will wreak havoc. Stay between the lines. This is the safe path to your destination.

Challenge #18

Where is your life out of balance? Use the above list if necessary to help you examine your life.

_____
_____

What must you do to get your life in alignment?

_____
_____

Have you drawn proper boundary lines in your spiritual life?

_____
_____

Personal life? (Time management, exercise, diet, hobbies, saying "no" to others)

_____
_____

Relational life? (In your relationships with others—parents, children, family, friends, co-workers, and social circle)

_____
_____

Financial life?
_____
_____

Professional life?
_____
_____

SOUL SEARCH AND RATE YOURSELF THE PAST SIX MONTHS
DAY 18: How do you rate when it comes to living a balanced life?

Go to the Baseline Data Table on DAY 30 and rate yourself.

DAY 19
GUARD YOUR HEART

***Guard your heart above all else,
for it determines the course of your life.***
Proverbs 4:23 (NLT)

* * *

Guard your heart. Sounds great, but what does that mean?

Your heart is the deepest part of you. It is where your desires, dreams, and affections reside.

Matthew 12:35 tells us:

A good man brings good things out of the good stored up in him, and an evil man brings evil things out of the evil stored up in him.

Here's a newsflash: You are responsible for what is in your heart.

The Bible gives directives on guarding your heart. This is by no means an all-inclusive list, but consider the following ways to guard your heart:

1.) Be careful what you put before your eyes: television, magazines, movies, and other media.

   I will not look with approval on anything that is vile. I hate what faithless people do; I will have no part in it. (Psalm 101:3)

2.) Resolve that you won't sin with your mouth.

> *You have proved my heart. You have visited me in the night. You have tried me, and found nothing. I have resolved that my mouth shall not disobey.* (Psalm 17:3, WEB)

3.) Guard your thoughts.

> *May the words of my mouth and the meditation of my heart be pleasing in your sight, O Lord, my Rock and my Redeemer.* (Psalm 19:14, NIV 1984)

4.) Deal with sin immediately and don't allow it room in your heart.

> *If I had cherished sin in my heart, the Lord would not have listened.* (Psalm 66:18)

5.) Get rid of pride.

> *The Lord detests all the proud of heart. Be sure of this: They will not go unpunished.* (Proverbs 16:5)

6.) Be careful to lead a blameless life.

> *I will be careful to lead a blameless life—when will you come to me? I will conduct the affairs of my house with a blameless heart.* (Psalm 101:2)

7.) Be careful who you let into your heart.

> *Guard your heart above all else, for it determines the course of your life.* (Proverbs 4:23, NLT)

Guarding your heart is an active, not passive, pursuit. The truth is, if you are not vigilant in guarding your heart, you can probably assume that the contents of your heart are not good. This isn't being negative; it's being realistic. Don't let just anything in your heart. Guard it with your life!

Challenge #19

Look back at the past six months and analyze what has come out of your heart.

Thoughts:_____
_____
_____
_____
_____

Attitudes:_____
_____
_____
_____
_____

Actions:_____
_____
_____
_____
_____

Words:_____
_____
_____
_____
_____

SOUL SEARCH AND RATE YOURSELF THE PAST SIX MONTHS
DAY 19: Is your heart bringing up good things?

Go to the Baseline Data Table on DAY 30 and rate yourself.

DAY 20
NO COMPROMISE:
LIVING BY YOUR CONSCIENCE

For since the creation of the world God's invisible qualities—his eternal power and divine nature—have been clearly seen, being understood from what has been made, so that people are without excuse.
Romans 1:20

* * *

God has placed a wonderful gift inside every man, woman, boy, and girl. That gift is a conscience. Our conscience is like an inner compass that shows where true north is. It points us to God's laws and principles.

Unfortunately, we don't hear much talk these days about living by our conscience, and most people are so out of touch with the conscience that they don't even know they have one, let alone how to hear and obey it. First Timothy 4:2 says we can sear our conscience in such a way that we make it numb. But according to Romans 1 and 2, God has placed His law in our hearts via our conscience, and we will all be held accountable for obeying that law.

Romans 1:20 tells us that God's invisible qualities are clearly seen, so no one will be excused for disobeying God.

What about the tribal person deep in the jungle of Africa who never hears the gospel of Jesus Christ? How can she be held responsible when she has never been given a chance for repentance? Have you ever asked yourself that question? I know I have. Romans 2:13-15 gives us the answer:

For it is not those who hear the law who are righteous in God's sight, but it is those who obey the law who will be declared righteous. (Indeed, when

Gentiles, who do not have the law, do by nature things required by the law, they are a law for themselves, even though they do not have the law. They show that the requirements of the law are written on their hearts, their consciences also bearing witness, and their thoughts sometimes accusing them and at other times even defending them.)

Although everyone will be judged by their adherence to their conscience, that doesn't give Christians a pass in sharing the gospel. We still have the responsibility to preach the gospel.

He said to them, "Go into all the world and preach the gospel to all creation."
Mark 16:15

Are you living by your conscience on a day-to-day basis regarding the little things as well as the big things? Take a moment and examine your adherence to your conscience.

Challenge #20

1.) Do you have a guilty conscience?

_____

Hebrews 10:22 gives the antidote:

Let us draw near to God with a sincere heart and with the full assurance that faith brings, having our hearts sprinkled to cleanse us from a guilty conscience and having our bodies washed with pure water.

2.) Don't let go of a good conscience. 1 Timothy 1:19 says,

Holding on to faith and a good conscience, which some have rejected and so have suffered shipwreck with regard to the faith.

3.) Finally, make this your motto regarding your conscience:

So I strive always to keep my conscience clear before God and man.
Acts 24:16

SOUL SEARCH AND RATE YOURSELF THE PAST SIX MONTHS
DAY 20: Are you in the habit of listening to and then obeying your conscience?

Go to the Baseline Data Table on DAY 30 and rate yourself.

DAY 21
PATIENCE

Whoever is patient has great understanding, but one who is quick-tempered displays folly.
Proverbs 14:29

* * *

As I write this, I am just a few days away from my vivacious three-year-old's birthday. She is the big sister to a two-year-old, who is equally full of vim and vigor. I'm working on many areas of my character, but patience is one area I am challenged with almost hourly at times.

If you are a parent, you have probably thought and/or said on numerous occasions, "How many times do I have to tell you that?" Patience, it seems, is in short supply for me. God is using a 3- and 2-year-old to reveal an area of my character that is lacking. And my impatience doesn't stop here. I see it raise its ugly head when I'm in a hurry, waiting for others, or trying to get my "all-important" plans completed.

Who do we think we are? We're standing in line, waiting longer then we think is acceptable, when impatience rises up inside us. What's our response? Irritability, being short or rude, making a snide comment, or just walking away so we can find a friend to share our "social injustice" with.

Maybe this description doesn't describe you at all. Maybe your impatience is with yourself, other Christians who should know better, or even God. Is He working fast enough for you? Is He answering your prayers when you think He ought to? Are you in a trial or difficult circumstance that should have been over months or even years ago—so you think?

How does one acquire patience? Two ways. First of all, patience is part of the fruit of the Spirit produced by remaining in Christ, the vine. We talked about what this means on DAY 13.

The second way one acquires patience is simply to put it on. In other words, make a decision that you are going to be patient. Colossians 3:12 says,

Therefore, as God's chosen people, holy and dearly loved, clothe yourselves with compassion, kindness, humility, gentleness and patience.

Aren't you convinced that it's that simple for you to control your temper? Let me ask you a simple question. If you were in the middle of one of your impatience fits and someone whose opinion you respected arrived on the scene, could you change your attitude? Maybe you're about to go off on a clerk, and someone you want to impress walks up. You know you could change your behavior on a dime. The fact is, you can control yourself. The question is, do you want to?

If you desire to be a person of character, you can't ignore this area.

Challenge #21

How would you rate your patience on a scale of 1-10?

1   2   3   4   5   6   7   8   9   10

SOUL SEARCH AND RATE YOURSELF THE PAST SIX MONTHS
DAY 21: What is your level of patience?

Go to the Baseline Data Table on DAY 30 and rate yourself.

DAY 22
PERSEVERANCE

Therefore, since we are surrounded by such a great cloud of witnesses, let us throw off everything that hinders and the sin that so easily entangles. And let us run with perseverance the race marked out for us.
Hebrews 12:1

* * *

Perseverance, simply put, is refusing to quit until you get the job done. This always involves suffering. It's not fun, never convenient, and usually lasts much longer than we think it should. It is, however, a link to character, as seen in Romans 5:3-4 (NIV 1984):

Not only so, but we also rejoice in our sufferings, because we know that suffering produces perseverance; perseverance, character; and character, hope.

The one thing you can count on is that perseverance will not disappoint. It always delivers. James 1:2-4 makes this clear:

Consider it pure joy, my brothers and sisters, whenever you face trials of many kinds, because you know that the testing of your faith produces perseverance. Let perseverance finish its work so that you may be mature and complete, not lacking anything.

Challenge # 22

Mature and complete, not lacking anything. Is that your desire? If so, what unfinished business is there in your life that you need to see to completion? A relationship, overcoming an addiction or bad habit? Forming a new habit? Finishing a project, goal, assignment, or job?

_____
_____
_____
_____
_____
_____
_____
_____

Start running the race today, but remember this: you're running a marathon, not a sprint. Pace yourself and keep your eyes on the finish line.

SOUL SEARCH AND RATE YOURSELF THE PAST SIX MONTHS
DAY 22: Are you a finisher?

Go to the Baseline Data Table on DAY 30 and rate yourself.

DAY 23
FAITHFULNESS

Many claim to have unfailing love, but a faithful person who can find?
Proverbs 20:6

* * *

A true mark of a person of character is faithfulness. This quality is not acquired automatically. It costs greatly, requiring constant attention and discipline. However, the returns are worth the investment. Faithfulness pays great dividends. Proverbs 3:3-4 says this about faithfulness:

Let love and faithfulness never leave you; bind them around your neck, write them on the tablet of your heart. Then you will win favor and a good name in the sight of God and man.

Here's what Proverbs 28:20 says about faithfulness:

A faithful person will be richly blessed, but one eager to get rich will not go unpunished.

Because faithfulness is such a broad characteristic with many dimensions, we will take a close look at the definitions of "faithful" from www.dictionary.com

Faith-ful
–adjective

1. strict or thorough in the performance of duty: *a faithful worker*.
2. true to one's word, promises, vows, etc.
3. steady in allegiance or affection; loyal; constant: *faithful friends*.
4. reliable, trusted, or believed.
5. adhering or true to fact, a standard, or an original; accurate: *a faithful account; a faithful copy*.
6. full of faith; believing.

The Merriam-Webster Dictionary gives the following synonyms for the word "faithful":

Synonyms:
1, 3. true, devoted, staunch. *3.* FAITHFUL, CONSTANT, LOYAL imply qualities of stability, dependability, and devotion. FAITHFUL implies long-continued and steadfast fidelity to whatever one is bound to by a pledge, duty, or obligation: *a faithful friend*. CONSTANT suggests firmness and steadfastness in attachment: *a constant affection*. LOYAL implies unswerving allegiance to a person, organization, cause, or idea: *loyal to one's associates, one's country*. *5.* precise, exact.

Challenge #23

How faithful are you? Below you will find the definitions and synonyms of faithful. Place a checkmark in front of the qualities you possess. Use the unchecked aspects of "faithful" as your take-off point in your pursuit of faithfulness. In the blank, write one thing you can do to take the first step toward acquiring that particular trait.

☐ strict or thorough in the performance of duty: *a faithful worker*.
_____

☐ true to one's word, promises, vows, etc.
_____

☐ steady in allegiance or affection; loyal; constant: *faithful friends*.
_____

☐ reliable, trusted, or believed.
_____

☐ adhering or true to fact, a standard, or an original; accurate: *a faithful account; a faithful copy*.
_____

☐ full of faith; believing.
_____

Make it your ambition that when all is said and done, you hear God say:

... Well done, good and faithful servant! You have been faithful with a few things; I will put you in charge of many things. Come and share your master's happiness!
Matthew 25:21

SOUL SEARCH AND RATE YOURSELF THE PAST SIX MONTHS
DAY 23: How would those who know you and associate with you rate your faithfulness?

Go to the Baseline Data Table on DAY 30 and rate yourself.

DAY 24
LOVE

*And now these three remain: faith, hope and love.
But the greatest of these is love.*
1 Corinthians 13:13

* * *

Want to know how important love is?

Jesus replied: "'Love the Lord your God with all your heart and with all your soul and with all your mind. This is the first and greatest commandment. And the second is like it: 'Love your neighbor as yourself.'"
Matthew 22:37-39

Take a look in a Bible concordance. There is no other character trait I could find more references to than love. This is because God is love. Everything He is and does flows out of love. It is His very essence.

Is love a characteristic in your life? It may be easy to justify that some people are just more loving and are naturally inclined to show love and kindness. However, the Bible clearly tells us that love is something we choose to do. Take a look at the following scriptures:

And over all these virtues put on love, which binds them all together in perfect unity.
Colossians 3:14

Above all, love each other deeply, because love covers over a multitude of sins.
1 Peter 4:8

Challenge #24

Contrary to popular opinion and according to the Bible, love is a choice, not a feeling. What are practical things you can do today to put on love?

1. _____
2. _____
3. _____
4. _____
5. _____
6. _____
7. _____

SOUL SEARCH AND RATE YOURSELF THE PAST SIX MONTHS
DAY 24: What is your level of love?

Go to the Baseline Data Table on DAY 30 and rate yourself.

DAY 25
COMPANIONS

Do not be misled: "Bad company corrupts good character."
1 Corinthians 15:33

* * *

Want to see the type of person you are becoming? Take a look at the people you spend the majority of your time with. It's like looking at yourself in the mirror. Don't believe it? Look at Proverbs 27:17:

As iron sharpens iron, so one person sharpens another.

Are you spending your time with people you would like to emulate? In becoming a person of character, you may have to change the people you are spending your time with. Maybe you need to find some godly people who will hold you accountable. Or you might need to limit or greatly reduce the time you spend with some of your friends.

Challenge # 25

A Japanese proverb says, "When the character of a man is not clear to you, look at his friends." Take a good look at the people you spend your time with. Like it or not, they are sharpening you, either in a positive manner or a negative one. Is their sharpening making you a person of character or a person of less-than-ideal character? Fill in the following table:

PEOPLE I HANG OUT WITH	POSITIVE OR NEGATIVE INFLUENCE

SOUL SEARCH AND RATE YOURSELF THE PAST SIX MONTHS
DAY 25: Are you surrounding yourself with people of good character?

Go to the Baseline Data Table on DAY 30 and rate yourself

DAY 26
PRIDE

Pride brings a person low, but the lowly in spirit gain honor.
Proverbs 29:23

* * *

Pride. We all have to deal with it to some degree, but for some it is more of an issue than for others. Is pride a problem for you?

We are not talking about confidence or knowing you are competent, but rather an excessive sense of one's own importance or ability. Pride says,

- "I don't need you or your help."
- "I am better than you."
- "I don't need God."
- "I am self-sufficient."
- "I am more important than others."
- "My needs are more important than others' needs."

If you are prideful, God Himself will see to it that you are brought low:

I will break down your stubborn pride and make the sky above you like iron and the ground beneath you like bronze.
Leviticus 26:19

But after Uzziah became powerful, his pride led to his downfall.
2 Chronicles 26:16a

Pride goes before destruction, a haughty spirit before a fall.
Proverbs 16:18

The eyes of the arrogant will be humbled and human pride brought low.
Isaiah 2:11a

I will punish the world for its evil, the wicked for their sins. I will put an end to the arrogance of the haughty and will humble the pride of the ruthless.
Isaiah 13:11

    The antithesis of pride is humility. Humility is a choice. The Bible says it is something we put on as we would a piece of clothing.

Therefore, as God's chosen people, holy and dearly loved, clothe yourselves with compassion, kindness, humility, gentleness and patience.
Colossians 3:12

Challenge # 26

    On a scale of 1-10, how prideful have you been the past six months?

1   2   3   4   5   6   7   8   9   10

    How can you "clothe yourself with humility"? (Being willing to say "I'm sorry. I was wrong," not needing always to have the answer, etc.)

_____
_____
_____

Just remember this: You can do this the easy way (you humble yourself), or you can do this the hard way (God humbles you). Which will it be?

SOUL SEARCH AND RATE YOURSELF THE PAST SIX MONTHS
DAY 26: Rate your level of humility?

Go to the Baseline Data Table on DAY 30 and rate yourself.

DAY 27
GREED

Give, and it will be given to you. A good measure, pressed down, shaken together and running over, will be poured into your lap. For with the measure you use, it will be measured to you.
Luke 6:38

* * *

The Merriam-Webster dictionary describes greed as a selfish and excessive desire for more of something (such as money) than is needed.

Do you have an insatiable desire for any of the following?

- Money
- Clothes, cars, or any other material possession
- Prestige
- Power
- Recognition
- Success
- Popularity (for you or for your child)
- Being part of the "in" group
- Fit body
- Position in your field of work
- Sex
- Food
- Anything other than a deeper relationship with Christ

These things aren't necessarily bad per se, but making them your goal is.

Why is greed so bad? My guess is that greed is the antithesis of who Christ is: He came to lay down His life. What a mission. What a goal. Greed does just the opposite. In fact, greed's motto could be: "It's all about me."

John the Baptist understood this concept well when he said,

> *He must increase, but I must decrease. [He must grow more prominent; I must grow less so.]"*
> John 3:30 (AMP)

What's the solution to greed? Become a giver. When your focus becomes blessing others by giving of your time, money, and resources, you will have solved the problem of greed in your life. It is just that simple. And the paradox of giving is the more you give, the more you receive back.

Challenge # 27

Examine your life. Is there any area in which you have a selfish and excessive desire? Are you willing to turn your focus from yourself and onto God and others? Why not purpose to become a giver—giving of your money, time, talent, love, resources—and watch how God blesses you in return.

_____
_____
_____
_____

SOUL SEARCH ANDRATE YOURSELF THE PAST SIX MONTHS
DAY 27: Are you living a generous, selfless, and giving life?

Go to the Baseline Data Table on DAY 30 and rate yourself.

DAY 28
ARE YOU COMMITTED TO BEING A LIFELONG LEARNER?

I have fought the good fight, I have finished the race, I have kept the faith.
2 Timothy 4:7

* * *

If you have gone through *The 30-Day Character Challenge*, you no doubt have come upon areas in your life that need improvement. However, I hope you don't close the book and think that after Day 30 you are finished, because as long as you are living on this earth, you will need to make constant adjustments. I like to compare it to your automobile. Regardless of how well you take care of it, from time to time you have to take it in for oil changes, tune-ups, and repairs. And when you do, it's not a big deal. There's no drama. You don't say, "That does it! I'm trading in this vehicle for a different one! This is the third time this year I've had to change the oil!" You just expect it and plan for it.

The same should be true of your character. You need to plan on regular maintenance "tweaks." Sometimes those "tweaks" will be along the lines of an attitude adjustment. Sometimes it may be in the area of disciplining yourself. And like the adjustment made on your automobile, this doesn't have to be a big deal. You just make the adjustment and move on.

As we are wrapping up *The 30-Day Character Challenge*, I pray that you will determine to be a person of character, regardless of the cost. Pursuing this lifelong endeavor will allow you to leave a legacy and say, as the Apostle Paul said,

I have fought the good fight, I have finished the race, I have kept the faith."
2 Timothy 4:7

Challenge 28:

Ask yourself if you will pursue character development for the rest of your life. This is not a passive activity. You won't automatically become a person of character. It will take hard work, commitment, and vision. Are you up for the challenge?

> **SOUL SEARCH AND RATE YOURSELF**
> *DAY 28: Are you willing to take on the assignment of character development and pursue it until you take your last breath?*
>
> **Go to the Baseline Data Table on DAY 30 and rate yourself.**

DAY 29
WHAT KIND OF PERSON WILL YOU BE IN FIVE YEARS?

A good man brings good things out of the good stored up in his heart, and an evil man brings evil things out of the evil stored up in his heart. For the mouth speaks what the heart is full of.
Luke 6:45

* * *

I've heard it said that two things that will determine the type of person you will be in five years: what you read and listen to, and the people you hang out with. That being said, what type of person will you be in five years?

_____
_____
_____
_____

Challenge # 29

What kind of person do you want to be in five years, and what changes do you need to make to become that person?

_____
_____
_____
_____
_____
_____
_____

> **SOUL SEARCH AND RATE YOURSELF THE PAST SIX MONTHS**
> **DAY 29:** Based on the decisions you are making, what kind of legacy will you leave?
>
>
> Go to the Baseline Data Table on DAY 30 and rate yourself.

DAY 30
BASELINE DATA

* * *

Whew! You made it! Now it's time to sit back and take a look at the baseline data you have been compiling day after day for the past thirty days. Remember, this is your baseline. It's a beginning point, not the end. Now you know where you are and where you need to be heading.

If you have not already done so, use the following table as a compilation of all the previous work you have already completed. You may want to re-record your results from time to time as a way to chart your course and see your progress.

Don't let the information you have recorded discourage you. Rather, use it as an impetus to spur you on to greater character development. You are the only one who will determine your destiny. The decision is in your hands. Will you leave a legacy of one who paid the price of developing her character?

\multicolumn{3}{c}{BASELINE DATA FOR *THE 30-DAY CHARACTER CHALLENGE*}		
DAY 1	Purpose of This Challenge	1 2 3 4 5 6 7 8 9 10
DAY 2	Truth about Self	1 2 3 4 5 6 7 8 9 10
DAY 3	Commitment to Change	1 2 3 4 5 6 7 8 9 10
DAY 4	Adopt a N.O.W. Philosophy (No Opportunity Wasted)	1 2 3 4 5 6 7 8 9 10
DAY 5	Motive	1 2 3 4 5 6 7 8 9 10
DAY 6	Admit You Are Helpless on Your Own	1 2 3 4 5 6 7 8 9 10
DAY 7	Personal Integrity Audit	1 2 3 4 5 6 7 8 9 10
DAY 8	Do Not Despise the Day of Small Beginnings	1 2 3 4 5 6 7 8 9 10
DAY 9	Resolve	1 2 3 4 5 6 7 8 9 10
DAY 10	Stewardship Fitness Test	1 2 3 4 5 6 7 8 9 10
DAY 11	Walking in Truth	1 2 3 4 5 6 7 8 9 10
DAY 12	Is Your Word Your Bond?	1 2 3 4 5 6 7 8 9 10
DAY 13	Self-Control	1 2 3 4 5 6 7 8 9 10
DAY 14	Self-Control: Thoughts	1 2 3 4 5 6 7 8 9 10
DAY 15	Self-Control: Words	1 2 3 4 5 6 7 8 9 10
DAY 16	Self-Control: Actions	1 2 3 4 5 6 7 8 9 10
DAY 17	Obedience Out of a Pure Heart	1 2 3 4 5 6 7 8 9 10

DAY 18	Appropriate Boundary Lines	1 2 3 4 5 6 7 8 9 10
DAY 19	Guard Your Heart	1 2 3 4 5 6 7 8 9 10
DAY 20	No Compromise: Living By Your Conscience	1 2 3 4 5 6 7 8 9 10
DAY 21	Patience	1 2 3 4 5 6 7 8 9 10
DAY 22	Perseverance	1 2 3 4 5 6 7 8 9 10
DAY 23	Faithfulness	1 2 3 4 5 6 7 8 9 10
DAY 24	Love	1 2 3 4 5 6 7 8 9 10
DAY 25	Companions	1 2 3 4 5 6 7 8 9 10
DAY 26	Pride	1 2 3 4 5 6 7 8 9 10
DAY 27	Greed	1 2 3 4 5 6 7 8 9 10
DAY 28	Are You Committed to Being a Lifelong Learner?	1 2 3 4 5 6 7 8 9 10
DAY 29	What Kind of Person Will You Be in Five Years?	1 2 3 4 5 6 7 8 9 10
DAY 30	Baseline Data— Pick One	1 2 3 4 5 6 7 8 9 10

Pick One

Let your eyes look right on [with fixed purpose], and let your gaze be straight before you. Consider well the path of your feet, and let all your ways be established and ordered aright.
Proverbs 4:25-26 (AMP)

    Going through this challenge, you likely will have identified many areas of your character that need improvement. That's good, but if we are not careful, it can be overwhelming to the point that we want to give up. That's why it's important to pick one thing to work on and then focus on that one thing. Don't worry if things don't change as quickly as you would like. As long as you are making forward progress, you are developing your character, and that is the whole point.

Take some time to talk to God about what He wants you to focus on. What area is He speaking to you about? Once you know where He is directing you, go with it. That is where His grace (His power) is in your life. Facing up to your weakness may not be easy. In fact, it may be downright frightening, but if you will partner with Him, you have this incredible promise:

Take my yoke upon you and learn from me, for I am gentle and humble in heart, and you will find rest for your souls. For my yoke is easy and my burden is light.
Matthew 11:29-30

Challenge # 30

What one thing are you going to focus on?
_____

What do you have to gain in becoming a person of character?
_____
_____
_____
_____

What do you have to lose in passing up the opportunity to become a person of character?
_____
_____
_____
_____

SOUL SEARCH AND RATE YOURSELF
DAY 30: Have you picked a character trait to work on and are committed to seeing it through?

Go to the Baseline Data Table on DAY 30 and rate yourself.

Notes

DAY 1 – PURPOSE OF THIS CHALLENGE

1. "McGwire Admits To Steroid Use." Associated Press. *The Chanute Tribune. 14 Jan. 2010: 1*

2. "Character," Merriam-Webster.com. http://merriam-webster.com/dictionary/character?show=0&t=1343407233 (accessed January 20, 2009)

3. Gough, Russell Wayne. *Character Is Destiny: The Value of Personal Ethics in Everyday Life.* Rocklin, CA: Forum, 1998. Print.

DAY 23 – FAITHFULNESS

4. "Faithful," Dictionary.com. 2009, http://dictionary.reference.com/browse/faithful?s=t (accessed March 29, 2009)

5. "Faithful," Merriam-Webster.com. http://merriam-webster.com/dictionary/faithful (accessed March 29, 2009)

www.ingramcontent.com/pod-product-compliance
Lightning Source LLC
LaVergne TN
LVHW051607070426
835507LV00021B/2820